FISH

superb ways with seafood

& shellfish

FISH

superb ways with seafood

& shellfish

contributing editor:
LINDA DOESER

HERMES
HOUSE

This edition published by Hermes House

Hermes House is an imprint of Anness Publishing Limited
Hermes House, 88-89 Blackfriars Road, London SE1 8HA
tel. 020 7401 2077; fax 020 7633 9499; info@anness.com

A CIP catalogue record for this book is available
from the British Library

Publisher: Joanna Lorenz
Cookery Editor: Linda Doeser
Copy Editor: Leslie Viney
Designer: Mason Linklater
Illustrator: Madeleine David

Previously published as '*Great Fish & Shellfish*'

© Anness Publishing Limited 1999 , 2004

1 3 5 7 9 10 8 6 4 2

NOTES

For all recipes, quantities are given in both metric and imperial measures and, where appropriate, measures are
also given in standard cups and spoons. Follow one set, but not a mixture, because they are not interchangeable.

Standard spoon and cup measures are level.

1 tsp = 5ml, 1 tbsp = 15ml, 1 cup = 250ml/8fl oz

Australian standard tablespoons are 20ml. Australian readers should use 3 tsp in place of 1 tbsp for measuring
small quantities of gelatine, cornflour, salt, etc.

Medium eggs are used unless otherwise stated.

CONTENTS

~

Introduction

Often called the "harvest of the sea," fish, shellfish and other seafood offer almost endless possibilities for delicious, nutritious and healthy meals. There are a vast number of different preparations for fish: grilled, baked, steamed, served in a creamy sauce, combined with fruit or vegetables, curried, wrapped in parchment or served cold in salads, to name just a few. The recipes in this book have been inspired by dishes from all over the world and explore interesting ways of cooking both familiar and unfamiliar varieties.

The book begins with an introduction to the main types of fish, with some helpful hints on buying and storing fish and useful equipment. This is followed by a step-by-step guide to techniques, including trimming, gutting, skinning, scaling, preparing steaks and cutlets and filleting. Techniques for seafood follow, with instructions for preparing mussels and clams, opening oysters and scallops and deveining shrimp. This section is completed with a guide to basic cooking techniques: poaching, steaming, grilling, and coating and frying. The recipes themselves are divided into seven chapters: Soups, Appetizers, Salads, Pasta and Rice, Fried and Grilled Dishes, Pies and Baked Dishes, and Casseroles and Stews.

Besides being easy and quick to prepare, seafood is highly nutritious and plays an important role in the modern cook's approach to preparing healthy meals. Modern research confirms the value of fish in the diet for lowering cholesterol levels, as well as offering many other health benefits.

More than anything else, fish—whether freshwater or from the sea— offers immense scope to the creative cook. The recipes here range from the simple yet delicious to the elaborate and self-indulgent. There are recipes to suit all tastes and budgets and dishes suitable for every occasion.

Types of Fish and Seafood

Fish can be almost any size and color and range from the solitary bottom dwellers in the deep ocean to the huge schools of coastal fish. However, from the cook's point of view, they fall into three categories: round fish, flat fish (both sea types) and freshwater fish.

Round fish

This large group, which includes such familiar varieties as herring, cod, haddock, whiting, pollack, anchovy, sprat, sardine, grouper and mullet, are distinguished by having a rounded body, eyes on either side of the head and by swimming with their dorsal (back) fin on top. As well as bony fish, it includes cartilaginous species, such as dogfish and shark. Round fish are usually sold whole, in fillets or in steaks. Many of the oily varieties, such as mackerel and tuna, are delicious grilled or fried. White fish, such as whiting, which has a particularly delicate flavor and fine texture, may be fried or poached. Firm-fleshed fish is ideal for baking or stuffing. Salmon are included in this group, although part of their life cycle is spent in fresh water.

Flat fish

This group, which includes sole (lemon and Dover), plaice, dab, flounder, turbot and halibut, swim on one side and have both eyes on the same side of the head. Usually the lower, blind side is paler than the upper side of the fish. Most flat fish, with the exception of halibut, turbot and skate, is sold whole or in fillets. The very large varieties are usually available as steaks, and only the wings of skate are sold. The shallow bodies of flat fish and their generally firm but tender and flavorful flesh make them ideal for grilling or sautéing.

Freshwater fish

Aside from trout, which nowadays is readily available as a farm fish, these are not so frequently seen as seawater fish. Favorite freshwater fish include bream, perch, St. Peter's fish, char, pike, carp, freshwater catfish and eel.

Crustaceans

This group covers all the aquatic creatures, both fresh- and sea-water, with five pairs of legs: lobster, crab, shrimp, crayfish and crawfish. They tend to have firm, sweet flesh and many have heavy front claws or pincers. The head and body are usually, but not invariably, enclosed in a tough shell or carapace. Shrimp are often sold cooked, although they are also available raw. Crabs and lobsters are fresher and more delicious if they are bought live, but some people find it distressing to kill them. Shrimp are especially delicious gently sautéed, while lobster is particularly suited to delicate poaching.

Shellfish

This group includes single-shelled mollusks, such as the whelk and periwinkle, and the more popular bivalves, such as oysters, mussels, clams and scallops. It also includes the family to which squid, cuttle-fish and octopus belong. Some shellfish, especially oysters, are usually eaten raw in their own juices from the shell. Cockles and razor shells may also be eaten raw, but are good in soups, too. Mussels and clams are delicious steamed in their own juices or in white wine and lemon juice, and scallops are

often poached. All shellfish should be bought on the same day it is going to be eaten as it turns bad extremely quickly.

Buying and storing

When choosing fish, it is the appearance and smell that reflect its condition. When buying whole fish, look for shining skin, bright color, pink gills and full bright eyes with black pupils and transparent corneas. The flesh should be soft but springy, and the body should be firm. Genuinely fresh fish has a clean, pleasant odor, so reject any with even a suggestion of a "fishy smell." The only exceptions are shark and skate. This is because their flesh contains a chemical that breaks down after death to yield ammonia, which has an irritating smell. It is best to store skate and shark for a couple of days after they have been caught before preparing and cooking.

Shellfish deteriorate more rapidly than fish. Many, such as clams and mussels, are sold alive for this reason. Cooked crab, lobster and shrimp are available, and some types of shellfish are sold frozen. However, neither has quite the same flavor and texture as fresh seafood. As a general rule, you can tell if seafood is fresh because it does not smell.

Seafood will stay fresh for no longer than one day if stored in the refrigerator. Wrap it loosely in waxed paper or foil to prevent its smell from penetrating other foods. Fish freezes well, but you should be sure that it really is fresh and has not already been frozen on the fishing ship and thawed before sale.

Equipment

Clockwise from top left: fish grid for the barbecue, fish kettle, whole fish grid for the barbecue, fish terrine mold, divided fish lifter, scaler, large fish server, fish server, fish platter, filleting knife, strong scissors, oyster knife, zester, skewers, fish-shaped mousse mold.

Divided fish lifter
A useful gadget that opens out so that you can lift a whole fish or large fillet of fish with one hand without breaking it.

Filleting knife
A long, flexible knife is essential for skinning and filleting fish, as it can curve around the shape of the body, its bones and flesh. Keep the knife as sharp as possible.

Fish grid for the barbecue
This circular grid is ideal for cooking whole small fish, such as sardines, on the barbecue. Place the fish in the shaped grid and position on the barbecue, turning the whole grid over halfway through the cooking time.

Fish kettle
This elongated saucepan, fitted with a trivet or rack, is used to poach large, whole fish, such as salmon. Place the fish on the trivet with water in the base of the kettle and make sure that the lid is tight fitting. Poach on the stove or in the oven. Kettles are available in different sizes and there is even a specially shaped kettle made for poaching turbot, but this is really not essential equipment for a domestic kitchen.

Fish platter
A large flat platter essential for displaying whole fish. It makes an attractive centerpiece, particularly on a buffet table.

Fish server
Good for lifting fish fillets or single portions of fish.

Fish terrine mold
Ideal for large fish pâtés or terrines. Always cook in a *bain marie*: in other words, placed in a large roasting pan, filled halfway up the side of the terrine mold with boiling water. Cast iron molds are ideal for cooking the terrine, but make sure that they are always covered with the lid and line the mold with waxed paper to make removal easy. Serve the terrine sliced.

Fish-shaped mousse mold
An attractive way to present a cold mousse or fish mold.

Large fish server
Useful for lifting whole fish and large fillets lengthwise.

Oyster knife
A tool made expressly for opening tightly closed oyster shells. You can pry the shells apart with the strong blade.

Scaler
This is perfect for scraping off stubborn scales. Alternatively, you can use a blunt knife. In either case, this is best done under running water.

Skewers
Use to cook brochettes on the barbecue or under the broiler.

Strong scissors
Good for trimming fins and tails.

Whole fish grid for the barbecue
This is designed for cooking a whole large fish on the barbecue. Gut before cooking and season well. Wrap in large sprigs of fresh herbs, such as rosemary. Turn over halfway through the cooking time.

Zester
A quick method to add citrus fruit zest to any stuffing or marinade or to make a quick, fresh garnish.

Trimming Round Fish

1 With a pair of heavy scissors, cut off the fins on either side of the fish, then cut away the ventral or belly fins.

2 Cut off the dorsal fins along the back.

3 Trim the tail by cutting a "V" shape into it.

Gutting Round Fish Through the Stomach

1 With a medium knife, slit the underside of the fish from the gills to the small ventral opening. Take care not to insert the knife too far.

2 Carefully loosen the stomach contents from the cavity with your fingers and pull them out.

3 Using a teaspoon, scrape along the vertebrae in the cavity to remove the kidney.

4 Pull out the gills. Wash the cavity with cold water.

Gutting Round Fish

1 With a heavy pair of scissors, cut along the fish's belly.

2 Remove the insides with your fingers and wash the cavity.

Boning Round Fish for Stuffing

1 Gut the fish through the stomach as described on the previous page.

2 Slit the fish on either side of the backbone, cutting the flesh away from the bone until it is completely detached.

3 With a heavy pair of scissors, snip the backbone once at the head and once at the tail.

4 Carefully lift out the backbone and discard.

Boning a Round Fish Through the Stomach

1 Gut the fish through the stomach as previously described. Continue the stomach slit on one side of the backbone as far as the tail.

2 Open the cavity and remove the insides.

3 Clean the insides of the fish, wiping away any remaining blood or guts.

4 Open the cavity and, with the blade of the knife, cut away the loose inside bones that line the flesh.

5 Turn the fish over and slit the flesh at the base of the backbone on the other side.

6 With the blade of the knife, cut loose the inside bones lining the flesh in the same way as the first side.

7 Carefully loosen the backbone of the fish completely.

8 With scissors, snip the backbone at the head and the tail.

9 Carefully peel the backbone away from the flesh with any inside bones.

10 The head can be kept and the two side fillets rolled in spirals, skin side inward. Alternatively, fold the skin outward and tuck the tail inside.

11 Alternatively, the head and skin can be removed and the fillets rolled or cooked flat.

Cutting Steaks and Cutlets

1 With a large, sharp knife, slice the fish across, at a right angle to the backbone, into slices of the desired thickness.

2 If necessary, cut through the backbone with kitchen scissors or a knife with a serrated blade.

C O O K ' S   T I P

Round fish and large flat fish, such as halibut, are often cut into steaks and cutlets for cooking. Steaks are cut from the tail end of the fish, while cutlets are cut from the center. They are usually cut about 1–1½ inches thick.

Filleting Round Fish

1 Holding the knife horizontally, slit the skin from head to tail along one side of the backbone.

2 Cut down to the backbone just behind the fish's head.

3 Holding the knife flat and keeping the blade in contact with the bone, cut off the flesh from head to tail in a continuous slicing motion.

4 Cut the backbone at the tail end with scissors.

5 Trim off the tail.

6 Cut the fish into two fillets.

Mussel Bisque

Served hot, this makes a delicious and very filling soup, perfect for a light lunchtime meal. It is also excellent cold.

INGREDIENTS

Serves 6

1½ pounds fresh mussels in their shells
⅔ cup dry white wine or dry cider
2 cups water
2 tablespoons butter
1 small red onion, chopped
1 small leek, thinly sliced
1 carrot, finely diced
2 tomatoes, skinned, seeded and
    chopped
2 garlic cloves, crushed
1 tablespoon chopped fresh parsley
1 tablespoon chopped fresh basil
1 celery stalk, finely sliced
½ red bell pepper, seeded and chopped
1 cup whipping cream
salt and freshly ground black pepper

1 Scrub the mussels and pull off the beards. Discard any with broken shells or any that do not close when sharply tapped. Place them in a large pan with half the wine and ⅔ cup of the water.

2 Cover and cook the mussels over high heat until they open up. (Discard any that do not open.) Transfer the mussels with a draining spoon to another dish and set aside until cool enough to handle. Remove the mussels from their shells, leaving a few in their shells to garnish, if desired.

3 Strain the cooking liquid through a clean piece of muslin or a fine cloth to remove any traces of sand or grit. Heat the butter in the same large pan and cook the onion, leek, carrot, tomatoes and garlic over high heat for 2–3 minutes.

4 Reduce the heat and cook for another 2–3 minutes, then add the cooking liquid, remaining water and wine, the parsley and basil and simmer for another 10 minutes. Add the mussels, celery, red pepper, cream and seasoning to taste. Serve hot or cold.

Seafood Soup with Rouille

This is a really chunky, aromatic mixed-fish soup from France, flavored with plenty of saffron and herbs. Rouille, a fiery hot paste, is served separately for everyone to swirl into their soup to flavor.

INGREDIENTS

Serves 6

3 red mullet, scaled and gutted

12 large raw or cooked shrimp

1½ pounds white fish, such as cod, haddock, halibut or monkfish

8 ounces fresh mussels

1 onion, quartered

5 cups water

1 teaspoon saffron strands

1 tablespoon boiling water

5 tablespoons olive oil

1 fennel bulb, roughly chopped

4 garlic cloves, crushed

3 strips orange rind

4 thyme sprigs

1½ pounds tomatoes or 1 can (14 ounces) chopped tomatoes

2 tablespoons sun-dried tomato paste

3 bay leaves

salt and freshly ground black pepper

For the rouille

1 red bell pepper, seeded and chopped

1 red chili, seeded and sliced

2 garlic cloves, chopped

5 tablespoons olive oil

¼ cup fresh bread crumbs

1 To make the rouille, process the pepper, chili, garlic, oil and bread crumbs in a blender or food processor until smooth. Transfer to a serving dish and chill.

2 Fillet the mullet by cutting off the flesh from either side of the backbone, reserving the heads and bones. Cut the fillets into small chunks. Peel half the shrimp and reserve the trimmings to make the stock. Skin the white fish, discarding any bones, and cut the flesh into large chunks. Scrub the mussels well, discarding any damaged ones and any that do not close immediately when tapped sharply with the back of a knife.

3 Put the fish trimmings and shrimp trimmings in a saucepan with the onion and water. Bring to a boil, then simmer gently for 30 minutes. Cool slightly and strain.

4 Soak the saffron in the boiling water. Heat 2 tablespoons of the olive oil in a large sauté pan or saucepan. Add the mullet and white fish and fry over high heat for 1 minute. Drain.

5 Heat the remaining oil and fry the fennel, garlic, orange rind and thyme until beginning to color. Measure the strained stock and add water until you have 5 cups of liquid.

6 If using fresh tomatoes, plunge them into boiling water for 30 seconds, then refresh in cold water. Skin and chop. Add the stock to the pan with the saffron, tomatoes, sun-dried tomato paste and bay leaves. Season to taste. Bring almost to a boil, lower the heat, then simmer gently, covered, for 20 minutes.

7 Stir in the mullet, white fish and shrimp, peeled and unpeeled, and add the mussels. Cover the pan and cook for 3–4 minutes. Discard any mussels that do not open. Serve the soup hot with the rouille.

COOK'S TIP

To save time, order the fish and ask the fishmonger to fillet the mullet for you.

Spiced Mussel Soup

Chunky and colorful, this Turkish fish soup is similar to a chowder in its consistency. It is flavored with harissa sauce, more familiar in North African cooking.

INGREDIENTS

Serves 6

3–3½ pounds fresh mussels

⅔ cup white wine

3 tomatoes

2 tablespoons olive oil

1 onion, finely chopped

2 garlic cloves, crushed

2 celery stalks, thinly sliced

bunch of scallions, thinly sliced

1 potato, diced

1½ teaspoons harissa sauce

3 tablespoons chopped fresh parsley

freshly ground black pepper

thick yogurt, to serve

1 Scrub the mussels and remove the beards, discarding any with damaged shells or any open ones that do not close immediately when tapped sharply with a knife.

2 Bring the wine to a boil in a large saucepan. Add the mussels and cover with a lid. Cook for 4–5 minutes, until the mussels have opened fully. Discard any mussels that remain closed. Drain the mussels, reserving the cooking liquid. Strain the cooking liquid through a clean piece of muslin or fine cloth to remove any traces of grit. Reserve a few of the mussels in their shells for a garnish and shell the remainder.

3 Plunge the tomatoes into boiling water for 30 seconds, then refresh in cold water. Skin and dice them. Heat the olive oil in a heavy pan and fry the onion, garlic, celery and scallions for 5 minutes, until golden.

4 Reserve a little of the onion mix. Add the shelled mussels, reserved liquid, potato, harissa sauce and tomatoes. Bring just to a boil, reduce the heat and cover. Simmer gently for 25 minutes or until the potato is breaking up.

COOK'S TIP

Harissa is a spicy purée made from peppers, cayenne, olive oil, garlic, coriander, cumin and mint.

5 Stir in the parsley and pepper and add the reserved mussels. Heat through for 1 minute. Garnish with the reserved onion mix. Serve hot with a spoonful of yogurt.

Fish and Okra Soup

The inspiration for this soup came from a traditional Ghanaian recipe. Chop the okra to achieve a more authentic consistency.

Serves 4

2 green bananas

4 tablespoons butter or margarine

1 onion, finely chopped

2 tomatoes, skinned and finely chopped

4 ounces okra, trimmed

8 ounces smoked haddock or cod fillet,
   cut into bite-sized pieces

3¾ cups fish stock

1 fresh chili, seeded and chopped

salt and freshly ground black pepper

chopped fresh parsley, to garnish

3 Add the fish, fish stock, chili and seasoning to the pan. Bring to a boil, then reduce the heat and simmer for about 20 minutes or until the fish is cooked through and flakes easily.

4 Peel the cooked bananas and cut into slices. Stir into the soup, heat through for a few minutes and then ladle into soup bowls. Sprinkle with the chopped parsley and serve.

1 Slit the skins of the green bananas, but do not peel. Place them in a large saucepan. Cover with water, bring to a boil and cook over medium heat for about 25 minutes or until the bananas are tender. Transfer to a plate and let cool.

2 Melt the butter in a large saucepan and sauté the chopped onion for about 5 minutes, until soft. Stir in the chopped tomatoes and okra and fry gently for another 10 minutes.

Noodle Soup with Pork and Szechuan Pickle

This soup is a meal in itself, and the hot pickle gives it a delicious tang.

INGREDIENTS

Serves 4

4 cups chicken stock

12 ounces egg noodles

1 tablespoon dried shrimp, soaked in
    water

2 tablespoons vegetable oil

8 ounces lean pork, finely shredded

1 tablespoon yellow bean paste

1 tablespoon soy sauce

4 ounces Szechuan hot pickle, rinsed,
    drained and shredded

pinch of sugar

2 scallions, finely sliced, to garnish

1 Bring the stock to a boil in a large saucepan. Add the noodles and cook until almost tender. Drain the dried shrimp, rinse them under cold water, drain again and add to the stock. Lower the heat and simmer for another 2 minutes. Keep hot.

2 Heat the oil in a frying pan or wok. Add the pork and stir-fry over high heat for 3 minutes.

3 Add the bean paste and soy sauce to the pork; stir-fry for 1 more minute. Add the hot pickle with a pinch of sugar. Stir-fry for 1 more minute.

4 Divide the noodles and soup among individual serving bowls. Spoon the pork mixture on top, then sprinkle with the scallions and serve immediately.

Snapper and Noodle Soup

Tamarind gives this light, fragrant noodle soup a slightly sour taste.

INGREDIENTS

Serves 4

8 cups water

2¼ pounds red snapper (or other red fish,
    such as mullet)

1 onion, sliced

½ cup tamarind pods

1 tablespoon fish sauce

1 tablespoon sugar

2 tablespoons vegetable oil

2 garlic cloves, finely chopped

2 lemon grass stalks, very finely chopped

4 ripe tomatoes, roughly chopped

2 tablespoons yellow bean paste

8 ounces rice vermicelli, soaked in warm
    water until soft

1 cup bean sprouts

8–10 basil or mint sprigs

¼ cup roasted peanuts, ground

salt and freshly ground black pepper

1 Bring the water to a boil in a saucepan. Lower the heat and add the fish and onion, with ½ teaspoon salt. Simmer gently until the fish is cooked through.

2 Remove the fish from the stock; set aside. Add the tamarind, fish sauce and sugar to the stock. Cook for 5 minutes, then strain into a bowl. Carefully remove all the bones from the fish, keeping the flesh in big pieces.

3 Heat the oil in a large frying pan. Add the garlic and lemon grass and fry for a few seconds. Stir in the tomatoes and bean paste. Cook gently for 5–7 minutes, until the tomatoes are soft. Add the stock, bring back to a simmer and adjust the seasoning.

4 Drain the vermicelli. Plunge it into a saucepan of boiling water for a few minutes, drain and divide among individual serving bowls. Add the bean sprouts, fish and basil or mint and sprinkle the ground peanuts on top. Fill up each bowl with the hot soup.

Crab and Egg Noodle Broth

This delicious broth is the perfect solution when you are hungry, time is short, and you need something fast, nutritious and filling.

INGREDIENTS

Serves 4

4 ounces fine egg noodles

2 tablespoons unsalted butter

1 small bunch scallions, chopped

1 celery stalk, sliced

1 medium carrot, peeled and cut into batons

5 cups chicken stock

¼ cup dry sherry

4 ounces white crab meat, fresh or frozen

pinch of celery salt

pinch of cayenne pepper

2 teaspoons lemon juice

1 small bunch cilantro or flat leaf parsley, to garnish

3 Add the chicken stock and sherry to the pan, bring to a boil, reduce the heat and simmer for another 5 minutes.

4 If using frozen crab meat, let it thaw. Flake the crab meat between your fingers onto a plate and remove any stray pieces of shell.

5 Drain the noodles and add to the broth, together with the crab meat. Season to taste with celery salt and cayenne pepper and sharpen with the lemon juice. Return to a simmer.

6 Ladle the broth into shallow soup plates, scatter with roughly chopped cilantro to garnish and serve.

1 Bring a large saucepan of water to a boil. Toss in the egg noodles and cook according to the instructions on the package. Cool under cold running water, drain and leave immersed in water until required.

2 Heat the butter in another large pan, add the scallions, celery and carrot, cover and soften the vegetables over low heat for 3–4 minutes.

Corn and Crab Meat Soup

This soup originated in the United States, but it has since been introduced into China. You must use creamed corn in the recipe to achieve the right consistency.

INGREDIENTS

Serves 4

4 ounces crab meat or chicken breast

2 teaspoons finely chopped fresh ginger

2 egg whites

2 tablespoons milk

1 tablespoon cornstarch paste

2½ cups vegetable or chicken stock

1 can (8 ounces) creamed corn

salt and freshly ground black pepper

finely chopped scallions, to garnish

1 Flake the crab meat (or roughly chop the chicken breast) and mix with the ginger.

2 Beat the egg whites until frothy, add the milk and corn-starch paste and beat again until smooth. Blend with the crab meat or chicken breast.

3 In a wok or saucepan, bring the stock to a boil, then add the creamed corn and bring back to a boil.

4 Stir in the crab meat or chicken breast and egg-white mixture, adjust the seasonings to taste and stir gently until well blended and the meat is cooked. Serve garnished with finely chopped scallions.

Main Course Spicy Shrimp and Noodle Soup

This dish is served as a hot coconut broth with a separate platter of shrimp, fish and noodles. Diners are invited to add their own choice of accompaniments to the broth.

INGREDIENTS

Serves 4–6

½ cup shelled, raw cashews

3 shallots, or 1 medium onion, sliced

2-inch piece lemon grass, shredded

2 garlic cloves, crushed

6 ounces spaghetti-size rice noodles,
    soaked for 10 minutes

2 tablespoons vegetable oil

½-inch square piece shrimp paste, or
    1 tablespoon fish sauce

1 tablespoon mild curry paste

1 can (14 ounces) coconut milk

½ chicken bouillon cube

3 curry leaves (optional)

1 pound white fish fillet, such as cod,
    haddock or whiting

8 ounces raw or cooked shrimp

1 small head lettuce, shredded

½ cup bean sprouts

3 scallions, shredded

½ cucumber, sliced and shredded

shrimp crackers, to serve

COOK'S TIP

To serve, line a large serving platter with the shredded lettuce leaves. Arrange the bean sprouts, scallions and cucumber in neat piles, together with the cooked fish, shrimp and noodles. Serve the salad with a bowl of shrimp crackers and the broth in a lidded stoneware pot.

1 Grind the cashews using a mortar and pestle or in a food processor with the shallots, lemon grass and garlic. Cook the noodles according to the instructions on the package.

2 Heat the oil in a large wok or saucepan, add the contents of the mortar or food processor, and fry for 1–2 minutes or until the nuts begin to brown.

3 Add the shrimp paste or fish sauce and curry paste, followed by the coconut milk, bouillon cube and curry leaves. Mix thoroughly and simmer for 10 minutes.

4 Cut the white fish into bite-size pieces. Place the fish and shrimp tails in a large frying basket, immerse in the simmering coconut stock, and cook for 3–4 minutes. Transfer the fish and shrimp tails to a serving platter with the salad and noodles and transfer the broth to a tureen or lidded pot and serve (see Cook's Tip).

APPETIZERS

Olive and Anchovy Bites

These melt-in-the-mouth morsels store very well; freeze them for up to 3 months or they can be kept in an airtight container for up to 2 weeks before serving.

Makes 40–45

1 cup flour

8 tablespoons (1 stick) chilled butter

4 ounces finely grated cheese, such as Manchego, aged Cheddar or Gruyère

1 can (2 ounces) anchovy fillets in oil, drained and roughly chopped

½ cup pitted black olives, roughly chopped

½ teaspoon cayenne pepper

sea salt

1 Place the flour, butter, cheese, anchovies, olives and cayenne in a food processor and pulse until the mixture forms a firm dough.

2 Wrap the dough loosely in plastic wrap. Set aside in the refrigerator to chill for 20 minutes.

3 Unwrap the dough and turn it out onto a lightly floured surface. Knead lightly and roll it out thinly.

4 Cut the dough into 2 inch wide strips, then cut across each strip diagonally, in alternate directions, to make triangles. Transfer to baking sheets and bake at 400°F for 8–10 minutes, until golden. Cool on a wire rack. Sprinkle generously with sea salt before serving.

COOK'S TIP

For a change, sprinkle the olive and anchovy bites with finely grated Parmesan cheese or dust lightly with cayenne pepper before baking.

Smoked Salmon Crêpes with Pesto

These simple crêpes take no more than 10–15 minutes to prepare and are perfect for a special occasion. Smoked salmon is delicious with fresh basil and combines well with toasted pine nuts and a spoonful of crème fraîche.

INGREDIENTS

Makes 12–16

½ cup milk

1 cup self-rising flour

1 egg

2 tablespoons pesto sauce

vegetable oil, for frying

scant 1 cup crème fraîche

4 ounces smoked salmon

¼ cup pine nuts, toasted

salt and freshly ground black pepper

12–16 fresh basil sprigs, to garnish

3 Heat the vegetable oil in a large frying pan. Spoon the crêpe mixture into the heated oil in small heaps. Allow about 30 seconds for the crêpes to rise, then turn and cook briefly on the other side. Keep warm. Continue cooking the crêpes in batches until all the batter has been used up.

4 Arrange the crêpes on a serving plate and top each one with a spoonful of crème fraîche.

5 Cut the salmon into ½-inch strips and place on top of each crêpe. Scatter each crêpe with pine nuts and garnish with a sprig of fresh basil.

1 Pour half of the milk into a mixing bowl. Add the flour, egg, pesto sauce and seasoning and mix to a smooth batter.

2 Add the remainder of the milk and stir until evenly blended.

Seafood Crêpes

The combination of fresh and smoked haddock imparts a wonderful flavor to the filling.

Serves 4–6

For the crêpes

1 cup flour

pinch of salt

1 egg, plus 1 egg yolk

1¼ cups milk

1 tablespoon melted butter, plus extra for cooking

2–3 ounces Gruyère cheese, grated

curly salad greens, to serve

For the filling

8 ounces smoked haddock fillet

8 ounces fresh haddock fillet

1¼ cups milk

⅔ cup light cream or half-and-half

2 tablespoons butter

¼ cup flour

freshly grated nutmeg

2 hard-cooked eggs, shelled and chopped

salt and freshly ground black pepper

1 To make the crêpes, sift the flour and salt into a bowl. Make a well in the center and add the egg and egg yolk. Whisk the eggs, starting to incorporate some of the flour from around the edges.

2 Gradually add the milk, whisking all the time, until the batter is smooth and has the consistency of thin cream. Stir in the melted butter.

3 Heat a small crêpe pan or omelet pan until hot, then rub around the inside of the pan with a pad of paper towels dipped in melted butter.

4 Pour about 2 tablespoons of the batter into the pan, then tip the pan to coat the base evenly. Cook for about 30 seconds, until the underside of the crêpe is golden brown.

5 Flip the crêpe over and cook the other side until lightly browned. Repeat to make 12 crêpes, rubbing the pan with melted butter between cooking each crêpe. Stack the crêpes as you make them between sheets of waxed paper. Keep warm on a plate set over a pan of simmering water.

6 Put the smoked and fresh haddock fillets in a large pan. Add the milk and poach for 6–8 minutes, until just tender. Lift out the fish using a slotted spoon and, when cool enough to handle, remove the skin and any bones. Reserve the milk.

7 Pour the light cream or half-and-half into a measuring cup, then strain enough of the reserved milk into the cup to make the total quantity of 2 cups.

8 Melt the butter in a pan, stir in the flour and cook gently for 1 minute. Gradually mix in the milk mixture, stirring continuously, to make a smooth sauce. Cook for 2–3 minutes, until thickened. Season with salt, pepper and nutmeg. Roughly flake the haddock and fold into the sauce with the eggs. Let cool.

9 Divide the filling among the crêpes. Fold the sides of each crêpe into the center, then roll them up so that the filling is completely enclosed.

10 Butter four or six individual ovenproof dishes and arrange 2–3 filled crêpes in each, or butter one large dish for all the crêpes. Brush with melted butter and cook in a preheated oven at 350°F for 15 minutes. Sprinkle on the Gruyère and cook for another 5 minutes, until the crêpes are warmed through. Serve hot with a few curly salad greens.

VARIATION

For variety, add cooked, peeled shrimp, smoked mussels or cooked fresh, shelled mussels to the filling, instead of the chopped hard-cooked eggs.

Sautéed Scallops

Scallops go well with all sorts of sauces, but simple cooking is the best way to enjoy their flavor.

INGREDIENTS

Serves 4

1 pound shelled scallops

2 tablespoons butter

2 tablespoons dry white vermouth

1 tablespoon finely chopped fresh parsley

salt and freshly ground black pepper

1 Rinse the scallops under cold running water to remove any sand or grit and pat dry using paper towels. Season them lightly with salt and pepper.

2 In a frying pan large enough to hold the scallops in one layer, heat half the butter until it begins to color. Sauté the scallops for 3–5 minutes, turning, until golden brown on both sides and just firm to the touch. Remove to a serving platter and cover to keep warm.

3 Add the vermouth to the hot frying pan, swirl in the remaining butter, add the parsley and pour the sauce over the scallops. Serve immediately.

Garlicky Scallops and Shrimp

Scallops and shrimp are found all along the Atlantic and Mediterranean coasts of France and are enjoyed in every region. This method of cooking is a typical Provençal recipe.

INGREDIENTS

Serves 2–4

6 large shelled scallops

6–8 large raw shrimp, peeled

flour, for dusting

2–3 tablespoons olive oil

1 garlic clove, finely chopped

1 tablespoon chopped fresh basil

2–3 tablespoons lemon juice

salt and freshly ground black pepper

1 Rinse the scallops under cold running water to remove any sand or grit. Pat them dry using paper towels and cut in half horizontally. Season the scallops and shrimp with salt and pepper and dust lightly with flour, shaking off the excess.

2 Heat the oil in a large frying pan over a high heat and add the scallops and shrimp.

3 Reduce the heat to medium-high and cook for 2 minutes, then turn the scallops and shrimp. Add the garlic and basil, shaking the pan to distribute them evenly. Cook for another 2 minutes until the scallops are golden and just firm to the touch. Sprinkle on the lemon juice and toss to blend.

VARIATION

To make a richer sauce, transfer the cooked scallops and shrimp to a warmed plate. Pour ¼ cup dry white wine into the frying pan and boil to reduce by half. Add 1 tablespoon unsalted butter, whisking until it melts and the sauce thickens slightly. Pour the sauce over the scallops and shrimp and serve.

Scallops Wrapped in Prosciutto

This is a delicious summer recipe for cooking on the barbecue.

INGREDIENTS

Serves 4

24 medium-size scallops, without corals, prepared for cooking

lemon juice

8–12 slices prosciutto

olive oil

freshly ground black pepper

lemon wedges, to serve

1 Preheat the broiler or prepare a charcoal fire. Sprinkle the scallops with lemon juice. Cut the prosciutto into long strips. Wrap one strip around each scallop. Thread them onto 8 skewers.

2 Brush with oil. Arrange on a baking sheet if broiling. Cook about 4 inches from the heat under a preheated broiler for 3–5 minutes on each side or until the scallops are opaque and tender. Alternatively, cook over charcoal, turning once, until the scallops are opaque and tender.

3 Set 2 skewers on each plate. Sprinkle the scallops with freshly ground black pepper and serve with lemon wedges.

COOK'S TIP

The edible parts of the scallop are the round white muscle and the coral or roe. When preparing fresh scallops, keep the skirt—the frilly part—for making stock.

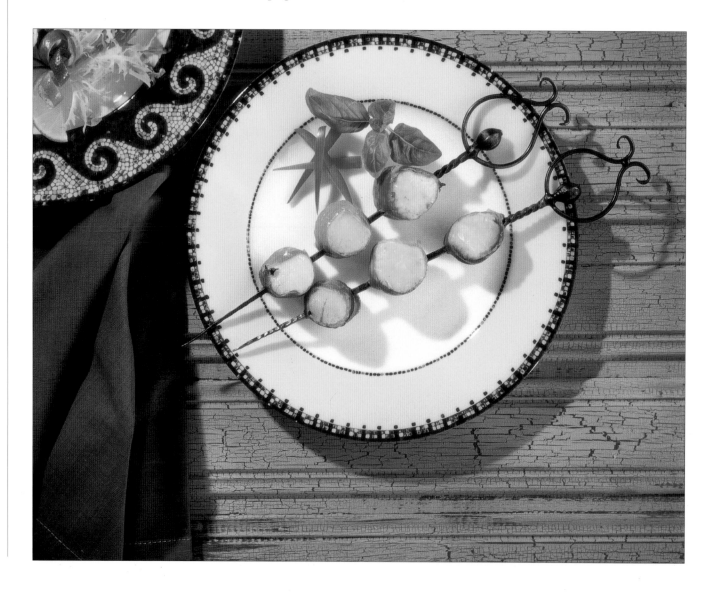

Mussels Steamed in White Wine

This is the best and easiest way to serve the small, tender mussels, bouchots, which are farmed along much of the French coastline. Serve with plenty of crusty French bread to dip in the juices.

INGREDIENTS

Serves 4

4–4½ pounds mussels

1¼ cups dry white wine

4–6 large shallots, finely chopped

bouquet garni

freshly ground black pepper

1 Discard any broken mussels and those with open shells that do not close immediately when tapped sharply. Under cold running water, scrape the mussel shells with a knife to remove any barnacles and pull out the stringy "beards." Soak the mussels in several changes of cold water for at least 1 hour.

2 In a large heavy flameproof casserole, combine the white wine, shallots, bouquet garni and plenty of pepper. Bring to a boil over medium-high heat and cook for 2 minutes.

3 Add the mussels to the casserole, cover tightly and cook, shaking and tossing the pan occasionally, for 5 minutes or until the mussels have opened. Discard any mussels that have not opened.

4 Using a slotted spoon, divide the mussels among 4 warmed soup plates. Tilt the casserole a little and hold for a few seconds to let any sand sink to the bottom and settle. Alternatively, strain the cooking liquid through clean muslin into a bowl.

5 Spoon or pour the cooking liquid over the mussels and serve immediately.

VARIATION

For Mussels with Cream Sauce, cook the shellfish as described here, but transfer the mussels to a warmed bowl and cover to keep warm. Strain the cooking liquid through a muslin-lined sieve into a large saucepan and boil for about 7–10 minutes to reduce by half. Stir in 6 tablespoons whipping cream and 2 tablespoons chopped fresh parsley, then add the mussels. Cook for about 1 more minute to reheat the mussels.

Grilled Sardines

Fresh sardines have plenty of flavor, so they are at their best when cooked in a simple way.

INGREDIENTS

Serves 4

8 sardines, about 2 ounces each

sea salt

2 lemons, halved, to serve

1 Gut the sardines, but leave on the heads and tails. With a sharp knife, slash each side of all the sardines diagonally three times.

2 Place the sardines on a broiler pan and sprinkle with sea salt. Cook under a broiler preheated to high for 4 minutes on each side, until the flesh is cooked and the skin is blistered and just beginning to char.

3 Transfer to a serving dish and serve immediately with the lemon halves to squeeze over.

Salt-cured Salmon

This delicious treatment is a good alternative to smoked salmon.

INGREDIENTS

Serves 10

½ cup sea salt

3 tablespoons superfine sugar

1 teaspoon chili powder

1 teaspoon freshly ground black pepper

3 tablespoons chopped fresh cilantro

2 salmon fillets, about 9 ounces each

flat leaf parsley, to garnish

garlic mayonnaise, to serve

2 Place one of the fillets, skin side down, in a shallow glass dish. Place the other fillet on top, with the skin side up. Cover with foil, then place a weight on top.

3 Chill for 48 hours, turning the fish every 8 hours or so and basting it with the liquid that forms in the dish.

4 Drain the salmon well and transfer to a board. Using a sharp knife, slice it diagonally into wafer-thin slices. Arrange on plates and garnish with sprigs of parsley. Serve with garlic mayonnaise.

1 In a bowl, combine the salt, sugar, chili powder, pepper and cilantro. Rub the mixture into the flesh of each salmon fillet.

COOK'S TIP

Make the most of the leftover salmon skin by turning it into delicious crunchy strips: After slicing the salt-cured salmon, scrape any remaining fish off the skin and discard. Cut the skin into ½-inch-wide strips. Fry for 1 minute in hot oil until crisp and browned. Drain on paper towels and let cool. Serve as a garnish for the salt-cured salmon or as a tapas dish in its own right.

Deep-fried Whitebait

A spicy coating on these fish gives this favorite dish a crunchy bite.

INGREDIENTS

Serves 6

1 cup flour

½ teaspoon curry powder

½ teaspoon ground ginger

½ teaspoon ground cayenne pepper

pinch of salt

2½ pounds fresh or frozen
    whitebait, thawed

vegetable oil, for deep-frying

lemon wedges, to garnish

1 Combine the flour, spices and salt in a large bowl.

2 Coat the fish in the seasoned flour and shake off any excess.

3 Heat the oil in a large heavy saucepan until it reaches a temperature of 375°F. Fry the whitebait in batches for 2–3 minutes until the fish is golden and crispy.

4 Drain well on absorbent paper towels. Serve hot, garnished with lemon wedges.

Sesame Shrimp Toasts

Serve about four triangles each with a soy sauce dip.

INGREDIENTS

Serves 6

6 ounces cooked shrimp, peeled
   and deveined
2 scallions, finely chopped
1-inch piece fresh ginger, grated
2 garlic cloves, crushed
½ cup cornstarch
2 teaspoons soy sauce, plus extra
   for dipping
6 slices stale bread from a small loaf,
   crusts removed
½ cup sesame seeds
vegetable oil, for deep-frying

1 Place the shrimp, scallions, ginger and garlic cloves into a food processor fitted with a metal blade. Add the cornstarch and soy sauce and work the ingredients into a thick paste.

2 Spread the bread slices evenly with the paste and sprinkle with the sesame seeds, making sure that they stick to the paste. Cut the slices into triangles and chill for 30 minutes.

3 Heat the oil for deep-frying in a large heavy pan until it reaches a temperature of 375°F. Using a slotted spoon, lower half the toasts into the oil, sesame seed side down, and fry for 2–3 minutes, turning over for the last minute. Drain on absorbent paper towels. Keep the toasts warm while frying the remainder.

4 Serve the toasts with the soy sauce for dipping.

COOK'S TIP

If you do not have a deep-fat thermometer, check that the oil is at the right temperature by tossing a stale bread cube into it. If it turns golden in 30 seconds, the temperature is just right.

Monkfish Parcels

These little dumplings of spiced fish taste delicious with the dressing of tomato oil.

INGREDIENTS

Serves 4

1½ cups flour

2 eggs

skinless monkfish fillet, 4 ounces, diced

grated rind of 1 lemon

1 garlic clove, chopped

1 small fresh red chili, seeded and sliced

3 tablespoons chopped fresh parsley

2 tablespoons light cream or half-and-half

flour, for dusting

salt and freshly ground black pepper

For the tomato oil

2 tomatoes, skinned, seeded and
finely diced

3 tablespoons extra virgin olive oil

2 tablespoons fresh lemon juice

1 Place the flour, eggs and ½ teaspoon salt in a food processor; pulse until the mixture forms a soft dough. Knead gently for 2–3 minutes, until smooth, then wrap in plastic wrap. Chill for 20 minutes.

2 Place the monkfish, lemon rind, garlic, chili and parsley in the clean food processor and process until very finely chopped. Add the cream, with plenty of salt and pepper, and process again to form a very thick purée.

3 Make the tomato oil by stirring the diced tomato with the olive oil and lemon juice in a bowl. Add salt to taste. Cover and chill.

4 Roll out the dough on a lightly floured surface and cut out 32 rounds, using a 1½-inch cookie cutter. Divide the filling among half the rounds, then cover with the remaining rounds. Pinch the edges tightly to seal, excluding as much air as possible.

5 Bring a large saucepan of water to the simmering point and poach the parcels, in batches, for 2–3 minutes, or until they rise to the surface. Drain and serve hot, drizzled with the tomato oil.

Crab and Ricotta Tartlets

Use the meat from a freshly cooked crab, weighing about 1 pound, if you can. Otherwise, look for frozen brown and white crab meat.

Serves 4

2 cups flour

8 tablespoons (1 stick) butter, diced

about ¼ cup ice water

1½ cups ricotta

1 tablespoon grated onion

2 tablespoons grated Parmesan cheese

½ teaspoon mustard powder

2 eggs, plus 1 egg yolk

8 ounces crab meat

2 tablespoons chopped fresh parsley

½–1 teaspoon anchovy paste

1–2 teaspoons lemon juice

salt and cayenne pepper

salad greens, to garnish

1 Sift the flour and a good pinch of salt into a mixing bowl, add the diced butter and rub it in with your fingertips, until the mixture resembles fine bread crumbs. Gradually stir in enough ice water to make a firm dough.

2 Turn the dough onto a floured surface and knead lightly. Roll out the pastry and use to line four 4-inch tartlet tins. Prick the bases with a fork, then chill in the refrigerator for 30 minutes.

3 Line the pastry shells with waxed paper and fill with baking beans. Bake in a preheated oven at 400°F for 10 minutes, then remove the paper and beans. Return to the oven and bake for another 10 minutes.

4 Place the ricotta, grated onion, Parmesan and mustard in a bowl and beat until soft. Gradually beat in the eggs and egg yolk.

5 Gently stir in the crab meat and chopped parsley, then add the anchovy paste, lemon juice, and salt and cayenne pepper, to taste.

6 Remove the tarts from the oven and reduce the temperature to 350°F. Spoon the filling into the shells and bake for 20 minutes, until set and golden brown. Serve hot with a garnish of salad greens.

Crab Savory

This scrumptious, baked seafood dish is rich and creamy.

INGREDIENTS

Serves 4

2 tablespoons butter

1 small onion, finely chopped

½ cup fresh brown bread crumbs

8 ounces crab meat

⅔ cup sour cream

2–3 teaspoons prepared mustard

pinch of cayenne pepper

squeeze of lemon juice

½ cup finely grated Cheddar cheese

salt

1 Melt the butter in a saucepan over medium heat, then cook the onion gently for 2–3 minutes, until it is soft but not brown.

2 Stir the bread crumbs, crab meat, sour cream and prepared mustard into the onions. Add a generous sprinkling of cayenne pepper, lemon juice and salt to taste. Heat through gently, stirring carefully.

3 Spoon the crab mixture into a baking dish, sprinkle the grated cheese over the top and place under a preheated, hot broiler until golden and bubbling.

Smoked Mackerel Pâté

The pâté can be flavored with horse-radish, if desired.

INGREDIENTS

Serves 4

10 ounces smoked mackerel fillet, skinned

6 tablespoons sour cream

8 tablespoons (1 stick) unsalted butter, softened

2 tablespoons chopped fresh parsley

1–2 tablespoons lemon juice

freshly ground black pepper

endive leaves and parsley, to garnish

fingers of toast, to serve

1 Remove any fine bones from the mackerel fillet, then mash it with a fork.

2 Work the sour cream and butter into the mackerel until smooth. Stir in the parsley and add lemon juice and pepper to taste.

3 Pack the mackerel mixture into a dish or bowl, then cover tightly and chill for 6–8 hours or overnight.

4 About 30 minutes before serving, remove the pâté from the refrigerator to let it return to room temperature. To serve, spoon onto individual plates and garnish with endive leaves and parsley. Serve with fingers of toast.

COOK'S TIP

For a less rich (and lower-calorie) version of this pâté, substitute 7 ounces low-fat cream cheese or sieved cottage cheese for the sour cream.

Sole Goujons with Lime Mayonnaise

This simple dish can be rustled up very quickly. It also makes an excellent light lunch or supper.

INGREDIENTS

Serves 4

scant 1 cup mayonnaise

1 small garlic clove, crushed

2 teaspoons capers, rinsed and chopped

2 teaspoons chopped gherkins

grated rind and juice of 1 lime

1 tablespoon finely chopped
    fresh cilantro

1½ pounds sole fillets, skinned

2 eggs, beaten

2 cups fresh white bread crumbs

oil, for deep-frying

salt and freshly ground black pepper

lime wedges, to serve

1 To make the lime mayonnaise, combine the mayonnaise, garlic, capers, gherkins, lime rind and juice and chopped cilantro. Season with salt and pepper to taste. Transfer to a serving bowl and chill until required.

2 Cut the sole fillets into finger-length strips. Dip each strip first into the beaten egg, then into the bread crumbs.

3 Heat the oil in a deep-fat fryer to 350°F. Add the fish strips, in batches, and fry until they are golden brown and crisp. Drain well on paper towels and keep warm while you cook the remaining strips.

4 Pile the goujons onto warmed serving plates and serve with the lime wedges for squeezing lime juice onto them. Hand the sauce around separately.

Spicy Fish Rösti

You can also serve these fish cakes crisp and hot for lunch or supper with a mixed green salad.

INGREDIENTS

Serves 4

12 ounces large, firm waxy potatoes

12 ounces salmon or cod fillet, skinned
    and boned

3–4 scallions, finely chopped

1 teaspoon grated fresh ginger

2 tablespoons chopped fresh cilantro

2 teaspoons lemon juice

2–3 tablespoons sunflower oil

salt and cayenne pepper

cilantro sprigs, to garnish

lemon wedges, to serve

1 Cook the potatoes with their skins on in a pan of boiling salted water for 10 minutes. Drain and let cool for a few minutes.

2 Meanwhile, finely chop the salmon and put it into a bowl. Stir in the chopped scallions, grated ginger, chopped cilantro and lemon juice. Season to taste with salt and cayenne pepper.

3 When the potatoes are cool enough to handle, peel off the skins and grate the potatoes coarsely. Gently stir the grated potato into the fish mixture.

4 Form the fish mixture into 12 cakes, pressing the mixture together and leaving the edges slightly rough.

5 Heat the oil in a large frying pan and fry the fish cakes, a few at a time, for 3 minutes on each side, until golden brown and crisp. Drain on paper towels. Serve hot, garnished with sprigs of cilantro and with lemon wedges for squeezing the juice on top.

Ceviche

This makes an excellent appetizer. With the addition of sliced avocado, it could make a light summer lunch.

INGREDIENTS

Serves 6

1 pound mackerel fillets, cut into ½-inch
    pieces

1½ cups freshly squeezed lime or lemon
    juice

8 ounces tomatoes, chopped

1 small onion, very finely chopped

2 drained canned jalapeño chilies or
    4 serrano chilies, rinsed and chopped

¼ cup olive oil

½ teaspoon dried oregano

2 tablespoons chopped fresh cilantro

salt and freshly ground black pepper

lemon wedges and fresh cilantro sprigs,
    to garnish

stuffed green olives sprinkled with
    chopped cilantro, to serve

1 Put the fish into a glass dish and pour in the lime or lemon juice, making sure that the fish is completely covered. Cover and chill for 6 hours, turning once, by which time the fish will be opaque, "cooked" by the juice.

COOK'S TIP

∾

For a more delicately flavored ceviche, you can use a white fish, such as sole.

---

2 When the fish is opaque, lift it out of the juice and set it aside.

3 Combine the tomatoes, onion, chilies, olive oil, oregano and cilantro in a bowl. Add salt and pepper to taste, then pour in the reserved juice from the mackerel. Mix well and pour over the fish.

4 Cover the dish and return the ceviche to the refrigerator for about 1 hour to let the flavors blend. Ceviche should not be served too cold. Let it stand at room temperature for 15 minutes before serving. Garnish with lemon wedges and cilantro sprigs, and serve with stuffed olives sprinkled with chopped cilantro.

Glazed Garlic Shrimp

This is a fairly simple and quick dish to prepare. It is best to peel the shrimp, as this helps them to absorb maximum flavor. Serve with a salad as an appetizer or as a main course with a selection of vegetables and other accompaniments.

INGREDIENTS

Serves 4

1 tablespoon vegetable oil

3 garlic cloves, roughly chopped

3 tomatoes, chopped

½ teaspoon salt

1 teaspoon crushed dried red chilies

1 teaspoon lemon juice

1 tablespoon mango chutney

1 fresh green chili, chopped

15–20 cooked jumbo shrimp, peeled
   and deveined

fresh cilantro sprigs, 4 unpeeled, cooked
   jumbo shrimp and 2 scallions, chopped,
   to garnish

1 In a medium saucepan, heat the oil and add the chopped garlic cloves.

2 Lower the heat and add the chopped tomatoes along with the salt, crushed chilies, lemon juice, mango chutney and chopped fresh chili.

3 Finally, add the shrimp, turn up the heat and stir-fry them quickly, until heated through.

4 Transfer to a warmed serving dish. Serve garnished with fresh cilantro sprigs, unpeeled jumbo shrimp and chopped scallions, if desired.

COOK'S TIP

This is a very fiery dish—if you would prefer it less hot, carefully seed the chili before chopping and reduce the crushed chilies to a pinch.

Smoked Salmon Terrine with Lemons

Lemons can be cut and sliced in so many ways. This melt-in-the-mouth smoked salmon terrine gives a time-honored side dish an intriguing new twist.

INGREDIENTS

Serves 6

4 sheets of leaf gelatin

¼ cup water

14 ounces smoked salmon, sliced

1½ cups cream cheese

½ cup crème fraîche

2 tablespoons dill mustard

juice of 1 lime

For the garnish

2 lemons

piece of cheesecloth

raffia, for tying

2 Set aside enough of the remaining smoked salmon to make a middle layer the length of the pan. Chop the rest finely by hand or in a food processor. Beat together the cream cheese, crème fraîche and dill mustard with the chopped smoked salmon until everything is well combined.

4 Tap the pan to expel any trapped air. Fold over the overhanging salmon slices to cover the top. Cover with plastic wrap and chill for at least 4 hours.

5 Make the garnish. Cut 1 lemon in half horizontally. Wrap each half in a small square of muslin. Gather the muslin at the rounded end of the lemon and tie neatly with raffia.

1 Soak the gelatin in the water in a small bowl until softened. Meanwhile, line a 1-pound loaf pan with plastic wrap. Use some of the smoked salmon to line the pan, laying the slices horizontally across the base and up the sides and leaving enough overlap to fold over the top of the filling.

3 Squeeze out the gelatin and melt gently in a small saucepan with the lime juice. Add to the smoked salmon mixture and mix thoroughly. Spoon half the mixture into the lined pan. Lay the reserved smoked salmon slices on the mixture along the length of the pan, then spoon on the rest of the filling and smooth the top.

6 Cut a small "V" from the side of the other lemon. Repeat at ¼ inch intervals. Turn out the terrine, then slice. Garnish with muslin-wrapped lemons and lemon "leaves."

Char-grilled Squid

Enjoy these tender bites of succulent squid right off the barbecue.

Serves 4

2¼ pounds prepared squid
6 tablespoons olive oil
juice of 1–2 lemons
3 garlic cloves, crushed
¼ teaspoon chili flakes
¼ cup chopped fresh parsley
lemon slices, to garnish

1 Reserve the squid tentacles, then, using a small, sharp knife, score the flesh into a diagonal pattern.

2 Place all the squid in a shallow, non-metallic dish. To make the marinade, thoroughly combine the olive oil, lemon juice, crushed garlic and chili flakes in a bowl.

3 Pour the marinade over the squid and put in the refrigerator for a minimum of 2 hours, stirring occasionally.

4 Lift the squid from the dish and reserve the marinade. Cook the squid on a barbecue for 2 minutes on each side, turning them frequently and brushing with the marinade until the outside is golden brown and crisp, with soft, moist flesh inside. Put the squid in a serving dish.

5 Bring the remaining marinade to a boil in a small pan, stir in the chopped parsley, then pour it over the squid. Garnish with lemon slices and serve immediately.

Monkfish Brochettes

These brochettes are colourful as well as full of flavour.

Serves 4

1½ pounds monkfish, skinned and boned
12 strips bacon
2 small zucchini
1 yellow or orange bell pepper, seeded and
    cut into 1-inch cubes
saffron rice, to serve

For the marinade

6 tablespoons olive oil
grated rind of ½ lime
3 tablespoons lime juice
2 tablespoons dry white wine
¼ cup chopped fresh mixed herbs, such as
    dill, chives and parsley
1 teaspoon honey
freshly ground black pepper

1 To make the marinade, combine the olive oil, lime rind and juice, wine, chopped herbs, honey and pepper in a bowl, then set aside.

2 Cut the monkfish into 1-inch cubes. Stretch the strips of bacon with the back of a knife, then cut each one in half and wrap around the monkfish cubes.

COOK'S TIP

If you are using wooden skewers, soak them in cold water before threading the fish and vegetables, so that they do not char when the brochettes are cooking.

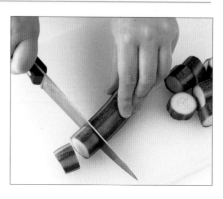

3 Pare strips of peel from the zucchini to create a striped effect, then cut into 1-inch chunks.

4 Thread the fish rolls onto skewers alternately with the zucchini and pepper. Place in a dish. Pour in the marinade and set aside in a cool place for 1 hour. Lift out the skewers, then broil for about 10 minutes, turning and basting occasionally with the marinade. Serve with saffron rice.

Thai Fish Cakes

Bursting with the flavor of chilies and lime, these little fish cakes make a wonderful appetizer.

INGREDIENTS

Serves 4

1 pound firm white fish fillets, such as cod
   or haddock
3 scallions, sliced
2 tablespoons chopped fresh cilantro
2 tablespoons Thai red curry paste
1 fresh green chili, seeded and chopped
2 teaspoons grated lime rind
1 tablespoon lime juice
2 tablespoons peanut oil
salt
crisp lettuce leaves, shredded scallions,
   fresh red chili slices, cilantro sprigs and
   lime wedges, to serve

1 Cut the fish into 1-inch chunks, then place in a blender or food processor.

2 Add the scallions, cilantro, red curry paste, green chili, lime rind and juice to the fish. Season with salt to taste. Process until finely ground.

3 Using lightly floured hands, divide the fish mixture into 16 pieces and shape each one into a small cake about 1½ inches across. Place the fish cakes on a plate, cover with plastic wrap and chill for about 2 hours until firm. Heat a wok over high heat until hot. Add the oil and swirl it around quickly to heat it.

4 Fry the fish cakes, a few at a time, for 6–8 minutes, turning them carefully, until they are evenly browned. Drain each batch on paper towels and keep hot while you are cooking the remainder. Serve on a bed of crisp lettuce leaves with shredded scallions, red chili slices, cilantro sprigs and lime wedges.

Seafood Wontons with Cilantro Dressing

These tasty wontons resemble tortellini. Water chestnuts add a light crunch to the filling.

INGREDIENTS

Serves 4

8 ounces cooked shrimp, peeled
   and deveined
4 ounces white crab meat
4 canned water chestnuts, finely diced
1 scallion, finely chopped
1 small green chili, seeded and
   finely chopped
¼ teaspoon grated fresh ginger
1 egg, separated
20–24 wonton wrappers
salt and freshly ground black pepper
cilantro leaves, to garnish

For the cilantro dressing
2 tablespoons rice vinegar
1 tablespoon chopped, pickled ginger
6 tablespoons olive oil
1 tablespoon soy sauce
3 tablespoons chopped cilantro
2 tablespoons finely diced red bell pepper

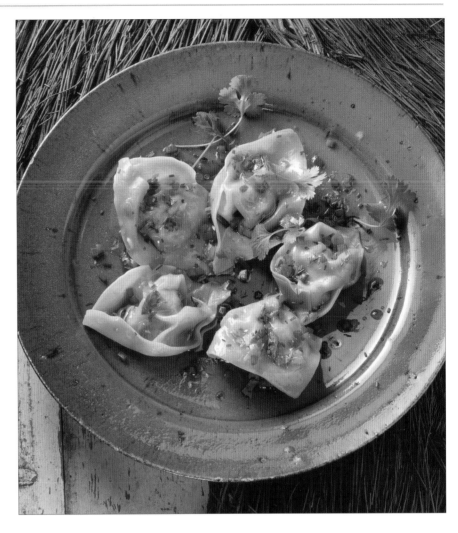

1 Finely dice the shrimp and place them in a bowl. Add the crab meat, water chestnuts, scallion, chili, ginger and egg white. Season with salt and pepper to taste and stir well.

2 Place a wonton wrapper on a board. Put about 1 teaspoon of the filling just above the center of the wrapper. With a pastry brush, moisten the edges of the wrapper with a little beaten egg yolk. Bring the bottom of the wrapper up over the filling. Press gently to expel any air, then seal the wrapper neatly in a triangle.

3 For a more elaborate shape, bring the two side points up over the filling, overlap the points and pinch the ends firmly together. Space the filled wontons an inch apart on a large baking sheet lined with waxed paper, so that they do not stick together.

4 Half fill a large saucepan with water. Bring to simmering point. Add the filled wontons, a few at a time, and simmer for 2–3 minutes or until the wontons float to the surface. When ready, the wrappers will be translucent and the filling should be cooked. Remove the wontons with a large slotted spoon, drain them briefly, then spread them on trays. Keep warm while you cook the remaining wontons.

5 Make the cilantro dressing by whisking all the ingredients together in a bowl. Divide the wontons among serving dishes, drizzle with the dressing and serve, garnished with a handful of cilantro leaves.

Grilled Green Mussels with Cumin

Green-shelled mussels have a more distinctive flavor than the small, black variety. Keep the empty shells to use as individual salt and pepper holders for fishy meals.

INGREDIENTS

Serves 4

3 tablespoons fresh parsley

3 tablespoons fresh cilantro

1 garlic clove, crushed

pinch of ground cumin

2 tablespoons unsalted butter, softened

¼ cup brown bread crumbs

12 green mussels or 24 small mussels, on the half shell

freshly ground black pepper

chopped fresh parsley, to garnish

1 Finely chop the fresh parsley and cilantro.

2 Beat the garlic, herbs, cumin and butter together with a wooden spoon.

3 Stir in the bread crumbs and freshly ground black pepper.

4 Spoon a little of the mixture onto each mussel and grill for 2 minutes. Serve garnished with chopped fresh parsley.

Welsh Rarebit with Anchovies

This classic snack or appetizer has been adapted and updated to include salty anchovies.

INGREDIENTS

Serves 4

1 can (2 ounces) canned anchovies,
   drained
12 tablespoons (1½ sticks) butter
6 slices of bread, crusts removed
4 large egg yolks
1¼ cups heavy cream
pinch of cayenne pepper
salt and freshly ground black pepper
1 tablespoon chopped fresh parsley,
   to garnish

1 In a food processor fitted with a metal blade, process the anchovy fillets with two-thirds of the butter. Toast the bread, spread with the anchovy butter, set aside and keep warm.

COOK'S TIP

If you find canned anchovies too salty, soak them briefly in cold water before processing them with the butter.

2 Melt the remaining butter in a small heavy saucepan and beat in the egg yolks.

3 Take off the heat and add the cream. Season to taste, then replace on a low heat. Stir until the sauce is thick. Pour onto the toast and sprinkle with the cayenne pepper. Garnish with the chopped fresh parsley.

SALADS

Spinach Salad with Bacon and Shrimp

Serve this hot salad with plenty of crusty bread for mopping up the delicious juices.

INGREDIENTS

Serves 4

7 tablespoons olive oil

2 tablespoons sherry vinegar

2 garlic cloves, finely chopped

1 teaspoon Dijon mustard

12 cooked jumbo shrimp

4 strips bacon

about 4 ounces fresh young
    spinach leaves

½ head oak leaf lettuce, roughly torn

salt and freshly ground black pepper

1 To make the dressing, whisk together 6 tablespoons of the olive oil with the vinegar, garlic, mustard and seasoning in a small pan. Heat gently until thickened slightly, then keep warm.

2 Carefully peel the shrimp, leaving the tails intact. Set aside.

3 Heat the remaining oil in a frying pan and fry the bacon until golden and crisp, stirring occasionally. Add the shrimp and stir-fry for a few minutes, until warmed through.

4 While the bacon and shrimp are cooking, arrange the spinach and torn oak leaf lettuce leaves on four individual serving plates.

5 Spoon the bacon and shrimp onto the leaves, then pour on the hot dressing. Serve immediately.

COOK'S TIP

Sherry vinegar lends its pungent flavor to this delicious salad. You can buy it at most large supermarkets and delicatessens.

Shrimp and Artichoke Salad

Artichokes are very popular in Louisiana, where this recipe comes from—and the local cooks are quite willing to use canned hearts.

INGREDIENTS

Serves 4

1 garlic clove

2 teaspoons Dijon mustard

¼ cup red wine vinegar

⅔ cup olive oil

3 tablespoons shredded fresh basil leaves
    or 2 tablespoons finely chopped
    fresh parsley

1 red onion, very finely sliced

12 ounces cooked peeled shrimp

1 can (14 ounces) artichoke hearts

½ head iceberg lettuce

salt and freshly ground black pepper

1 Coarsely chop the garlic, then crush it to a pulp with 1 teaspoon salt, using the flat of a heavy knife blade.

2 Mix the garlic and mustard to a paste, then beat in the vinegar and finally the olive oil, beating hard to make a thick, creamy dressing. Season with freshly ground black pepper and, if necessary, additional salt.

3 Stir the fresh basil into the dressing, followed by the finely sliced red onion. Let stand for 30 minutes at room temperature, then stir in the shrimp and chill in the refrigerator for 1 hour or until ready to serve.

4 Drain the artichoke hearts and halve each one. Shred the lettuce finely.

5 Make a bed of lettuce on a serving platter or 4 individual salad plates and spread the artichoke hearts over it.

6 Immediately before serving, pour the shrimp and sliced onion and their marinade on top of the salad.

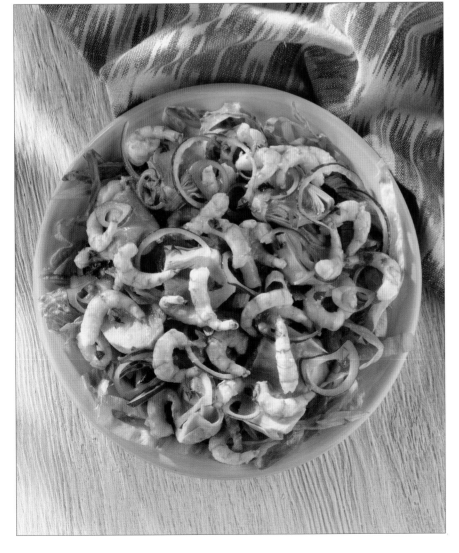

Grilled Salmon and Spring Vegetable Salad

Spring is the time to enjoy sweet young vegetables. Cook them briefly, cool to room temperature, dress and serve with a piece of lightly grilled salmon topped with sorrel and quails' eggs.

INGREDIENTS

Serves 4

12 ounces small new potatoes, scrubbed
   or scraped

4 quails' eggs

4 small carrots, peeled

1 can (4 ounces) baby corn

1 cup sugar snap peas, trimmed

1 cup fine green beans, trimmed

2 small zucchini

2 small patty pan squash (optional)

½ cup French dressing

4 salmon fillets, each weighing 5 ounces,
   skinned

4 ounces sorrel or young spinach,
   stems removed

salt and freshly ground black pepper

1 Bring the potatoes to a boil in salted water and cook for 15–20 minutes. Drain, cover and keep warm.

2 Cover the quails' eggs with boiling water and cook for 8 minutes. Refresh under cold water, shell and cut in half.

3 Bring a saucepan of salted water to a boil, add all the other vegetables, except the sorrel, and cook for about 3 minutes. Drain well. Place the hot vegetables and potatoes in a salad bowl, moisten with a little French dressing and let cool.

4 Brush the salmon fillets with French dressing and broil for 6 minutes, turning once.

5 Place the sorrel in a stainless steel or enamel saucepan with ¼ cup French dressing, cover and soften over low heat for 2 minutes. Strain and cool the sorrel to room temperature. Moisten the vegetables set aside in step 3 with the remaining dressing.

6 Divide the potatoes and vegetables between 4 large plates, then position a piece of salmon on one side of each plate. Finally, place a spoonful of sorrel on each piece of salmon and top with 2 halves of a quail's egg. Season to taste and serve at room temperature.

COOK'S TIP

For French dressing, combine 6 tablespoons olive oil, 2 tablespoons white wine vinegar, 1 teaspoon Dijon mustard, 1 teaspoon sugar, 1 crushed garlic clove and seasoning to taste.

Warm Salmon Salad

Light and fresh, this salad is perfect for an al fresco summer lunch. Serve it immediately, or you'll find the salad greens will lose their bright color and texture.

INGREDIENTS

Serves 4

1 pound salmon fillet, skinned

2 tablespoons sesame oil

grated rind of ½ orange

juice of 1 orange

1 teaspoon Dijon mustard

1 tablespoon chopped fresh tarragon

3 tablespoons peanut oil

1 cup fine green beans, trimmed

2 ounces mixed salad greens, such as
young spinach leaves, radicchio, frisée
and oak leaf lettuce

1 tablespoon toasted sesame seeds

salt and freshly ground black pepper

1 Cut the salmon into bite-size pieces, then make the dressing. Combine the sesame oil, orange rind and juice, mustard, chopped tarragon and seasoning in a bowl. Set aside.

2 Heat the peanut oil in a frying pan. Add the salmon pieces and fry for 3–4 minutes, until lightly browned but still tender inside.

3 Meanwhile, blanch the green beans in boiling salted water for about 5–6 minutes, until they are tender, but still crisp.

4 Add the dressing to the salmon, toss together gently and cook for 30 seconds. Remove the pan from the heat.

5 Arrange the salad greens on 4 serving plates. Drain the beans and toss over the leaves. Spoon over the salmon and cooking juices and serve immediately, sprinkled with the toasted sesame seeds.

Salmon and Tuna Parcels

You will need fairly large smoked salmon slices as they are wrapped around a light tuna mixture before being served on a vibrant salad.

INGREDIENTS

Serves 4

2 tablespoons low-fat plain yogurt
1 tablespoon sun-dried tomato paste
1 teaspoon whole-grain honey mustard
grated rind and juice of 1 lime
1 can (7 ounces) tuna in brine, drained
5 ounces smoked salmon slices
salt and freshly ground black pepper
fresh mint leaves, to garnish

For the salad

3 tomatoes, sliced
2 kiwi fruit, peeled and sliced
¼ cucumber, cut into julienne sticks

For the mint vinaigrette

1 tablespoon wine vinegar
3 tablespoons olive oil
1 tablespoon chopped fresh mint

COOK'S TIP

Although healthy eating guidelines recommend reducing the amount of fat, particularly saturated fat, in the diet, salad dressings made with polyunsaturated or monounsaturated oil, such as olive oil, can and should be included, in sensible moderation.
This recipe is not high in calories, but if weight control is a real issue, use an oil-free dressing instead of vinaigrette.

1 Mix the yogurt, tomato paste and mustard in a bowl. Stir in the grated lime rind and juice. Add the tuna, with black pepper to taste, and mix well.

2 Spread out the salmon slices on a board and spoon some of the tuna mixture onto each piece.

3 Roll up or fold the smoked salmon into neat parcels. Carefully press the edges together to seal.

4 Make the salad. Arrange the tomato and kiwi slices on 4 serving plates. Scatter on the cucumber sticks.

5 Make the vinaigrette. Put all the ingredients in a screw-top jar, season with salt and pepper and shake vigorously. Spoon a little vinaigrette over each salad.

6 Arrange 3–4 salmon parcels on each salad, garnish with the mint leaves and serve.

Avocado and Smoked Fish Salad

Avocado and smoked fish make an excellent combination and, flavored with herbs and spices, create a delectable salad.

INGREDIENTS

Serves 4

4 tablespoons (½ stick) butter

½ onion, finely sliced

1 teaspoon mustard seeds

8 ounces smoked mackerel, flaked

2 tablespoons chopped fresh cilantro

2 firm tomatoes, skinned and chopped

1 tablespoon lemon juice

salt and freshly ground black pepper

For the salad

2 avocado pears

½ cucumber

1 tablespoon lemon juice

2 firm tomatoes

1 green chili

1 Melt the butter in a frying pan, add the sliced onion and mustard seeds and fry for about 5 minutes, until the onion is soft, but not colored.

2 Add the fish, cilantro leaves, tomatoes and lemon juice and cook over low heat for 2–3 minutes. Remove from the heat and set aside to cool.

3 Make the salad. Peel and thinly slice the avocado pears and slice the cucumber. Put into a bowl and sprinkle with the lemon juice.

4 Slice the tomatoes. Seed and finely chop the chili.

5 Place the fish mixture in the center of a serving plate.

6 Arrange the avocado pears, cucumber and tomatoes around the fish. Alternatively, spoon a quarter of the fish mixture onto each of 4 serving plates and divide the avocados, cucumber and tomatoes equally. Sprinkle with the chopped chili and a little salt and pepper and serve.

Warm Fish Salad with Mango Dressing

This salad is best served during the summer months, preferably out-of-doors. The dressing combines the flavor of rich mango with hot chili, ginger and lime.

INGREDIENTS

Serves 4

1 loaf of French bread

4 black bream or porgy, each weighing about 10 ounces

1 tablespoon vegetable oil

1 mango

½-inch piece fresh ginger

1 fresh red chili, seeded and finely chopped

2 tablespoons lime juice

2 tablespoons chopped fresh cilantro

6 ounces young spinach

5 ounces bok choy

6 ounces cherry tomatoes, halved

1 Cut the French loaf into 8-inch lengths. Slice length-ways, then cut into thick fingers. Place the bread on a baking sheet and dry in a preheated oven at 350°F for 15 minutes. Slash the fish deeply on both sides with a sharp knife and moisten with oil. Cook under a preheated broiler or on a barbecue for 6 minutes, turning once.

2 Peel and pit the mango. Slice the flesh and place half of it in a food processor. Peel and finely grate the ginger, then add to the food processor with the chili, lime juice and cilantro. Process until smooth. Adjust to a pouring consistency with 2–3 tablespoons water.

3 Wash the salad greens and spin dry, then divide them equally between 4 serving plates. Place the fish on the leaves. Spoon on the mango dressing and finish with slices of mango and cherry tomato halves. Serve with the fingers of crispy French bread.

COOK'S TIP

Other fish suitable for this salad include salmon, monkfish, tuna, sea bass and halibut. Use fillets, cutlets or steaks.

Mediterranean Salad with Basil

A type of Salade Niçoise with pasta, this conjures up all the sunny flavors of the Mediterranean.

INGREDIENTS

Serves 4

8 ounces chunky pasta shapes

1 cup green beans

2 large ripe tomatoes

2 ounces fresh basil leaves

1 can (7 ounces) tuna fish in oil, drained and roughly flaked

2 hard-cooked eggs, shelled and sliced or quartered

1 can (2 ounces) anchovy fillets, drained

salt and freshly ground black pepper

capers and black olives, to garnish

For the dressing

6 tablespoons extra virgin olive oil

2 tablespoons white wine vinegar or lemon juice

2 garlic cloves, crushed

½ teaspoon Dijon mustard

2 tablespoons chopped fresh basil

1 Whisk all the ingredients for the dressing together, season with salt and pepper and let infuse while you make the salad.

2 Cook the pasta in plenty of boiling salted water according to the manufacturer's instructions. Drain well and set aside to cool.

3 Trim the green beans and blanch them in boiling salted water for 3 minutes. Drain, then refresh in cold water.

4 Slice or quarter the tomatoes and arrange on the base of a bowl. Moisten with a little dressing and cover with a quarter of the basil leaves. Then cover with the beans. Moisten with a little more dressing and cover with a third of the remaining basil.

5 Cover with the pasta tossed in a little more dressing, half the remaining basil and the roughly flaked tuna.

6 Arrange the sliced eggs on top. Finally, scatter over the anchovy fillets, capers and black olives. Pour on the remaining dressing and garnish with the remaining basil. Serve immediately. Do not be tempted to chill this salad—all the flavor will be dulled.

COOK'S TIP

Olives marinated in oil flavored with garlic, herbs and lemon peel would add an extra-special touch to this salad. Choose plump, black olives that are fully ripened. Marinated olives are available at large supermarkets and delicatessens, or you could prepare them yourself.

Thai Seafood Salad

This unusual seafood salad with chili, lemon grass and fish sauce is light and refreshing.

INGREDIENTS

Serves 4

8 ounces ready-prepared squid

8 ounces raw tiger shrimp

8 scallops, shelled

8 ounces firm white fish

2–3 tablespoons olive oil

small mixed lettuce leaves and cilantro
  sprigs, to serve

For the dressing

2 small fresh red chilies, seeded and
  finely chopped

2-inch piece lemon grass, finely chopped

2 fresh kaffir lime leaves, shredded

2 tablespoons Thai fish sauce

2 shallots, thinly sliced

2 tablespoons lime juice

2 tablespoons rice vinegar

2 teaspoons superfine sugar

1 Prepare the seafood. Slit open the squid bodies, cut into square pieces, then score the flesh in a crisscross pattern with a sharp knife. Halve the tentacles, if necessary. Peel and devein the shrimp. Remove the dark beard-like fringe and tough muscle from the scallops. Cube the white fish.

2 Heat a wok or large frying pan until hot. Add the oil and swirl it around, then add the shrimp and stir-fry for 2–3 minutes, until pink. Transfer to a large bowl. Stir-fry the squid and scallops for 1–2 minutes, until opaque. Remove and add to the shrimp. Stir-fry the white fish for 2–3 minutes. Remove and add to the cooked seafood. Reserve any juices.

3 Put all the dressing ingredients in a small bowl with the reserved juices from the wok or frying pan and mix well.

4 Pour the dressing over the seafood and toss gently. Arrange the greens and cilantro sprigs on 4 individual plates, then spoon the seafood on top. Serve immediately.

Gado Gado

Gado Gado is a traditional Indonesian salad around which friends and family gather to eat. Fillings are chosen and wrapped in a lettuce leaf. The parcel is then dipped in a spicy peanut sauce and eaten, usually with the left hand. Salad ingredients vary according to what is in season.

INGREDIENTS

Serves 4

2 medium potatoes, peeled

3 eggs

1½ cups green beans, trimmed

1 head romaine lettuce

4 tomatoes, cut into wedges

1 cup bean sprouts

½ cucumber, peeled and cut into fingers

5 ounces giant white radish, peeled and grated

6 ounces tofu, cut into large dice

12 ounces large cooked peeled shrimp

1 small bunch fresh cilantro

salt

For the spicy peanut sauce

½ cup smooth peanut butter

juice of ½ lemon

2 shallots or 1 small onion, finely chopped

1 garlic clove, crushed

1–2 small fresh red chilies, seeded and finely chopped

2 tablespoons fish sauce (optional)

⅔ cup coconut milk, canned or fresh

1 tablespoon superfine sugar

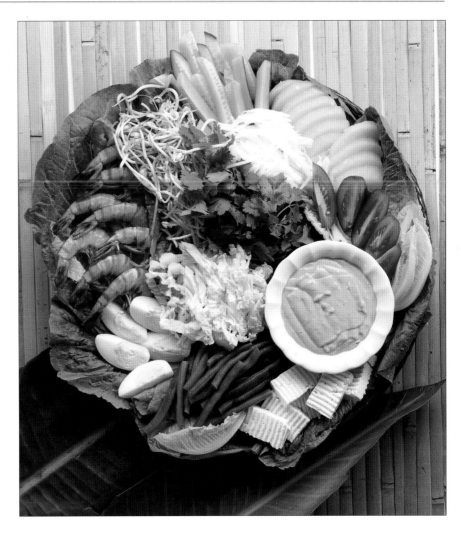

1 To make the peanut sauce, combine the ingredients in a food processor until smooth.

2 Bring the potatoes to a boil in salted water and simmer for 20 minutes. Bring a second pan of salted water to a boil. To avoid using too many pans, cook the eggs and beans in the same pan.

3 Lower the eggs into the boiling water in the second pan; then, after 6 minutes, add the beans in a steamer for another 6 minutes. (Hard-cooked eggs should cook for a total of 12 minutes.) Cool the potatoes, eggs and green beans under cold running water.

4 Wash and spin the lettuce leaves and use the outer leaves to line a large platter. Pile the remainder on one side of the platter.

5 Slice the potatoes. Shell and quarter the eggs. Arrange the potatoes, eggs, beans and tomatoes in separate piles. Arrange the other salad ingredients and the shrimp in a similar way to cover the platter. Garnish with the cilantro.

6 Transfer the spicy peanut sauce to an attractive bowl and bring to the table with the salad.

HANDLING CHILIES

Red chilies are considered to be sweeter and hotter than green ones. Smaller varieties of both red and green are likely to be more pungent than larger varieties. You can lessen the intensity of a fresh chili by splitting it open and removing the white seed-bearing membrane. The residue released when chilies are cut can cause serious irritation to the skin. Be sure to wash your hands thoroughly after handling raw chilies and avoid touching your eyes or any sensitive skin areas.

Seafood Salad with Fragrant Herbs

This tasty medley of seafood and noodles is a meal in itself.

INGREDIENTS

Serves 4–6

1 cup fish stock or water

12 ounces squid, cleaned and cut into rings

12 raw jumbo shrimp, peeled and deveined

12 scallops, cleaned

2 ounces bean thread noodles, soaked in
    warm water for 30 minutes

½ cucumber, cut into thin sticks

1 stalk lemon grass, finely chopped

2 kaffir lime leaves, finely shredded

2 shallots, finely sliced

juice of 1–2 limes

2 tablespoons fish sauce

2 tablespoons chopped scallion

2 tablespoons cilantro leaves

12–15 mint leaves, roughly torn

4 red chilies, seeded and sliced

cilantro sprigs, to garnish

1 Pour the fish stock into a medium-size saucepan, set over high heat and bring to a boil.

2 Place each type of seafood individually in the stock and cook for a few minutes. Remove and set aside.

3 Drain the bean thread noodles and cut them into short lengths, about 2 inches long. Combine the noodles with the cooked seafood.

4 Add the cucumber, lemon grass, kaffir lime leaves, shallots, lime juice, fish sauce, scallion, cilantro, mint leaves and chilies and combine well. Serve garnished with the cilantro sprigs.

Pomelo Salad

Pomelo is a large, pear-shaped fruit that resembles a grapefruit.

INGREDIENTS

Serves 4-6

2 tablespoons vegetable oil

4 shallots, finely sliced

2 garlic cloves, finely sliced

1 large pomelo

1 tablespoon roasted peanuts

4 ounces cooked peeled shrimp

4 ounces cooked crab meat

10–12 small mint leaves

2 scallions, finely sliced

2 red chilies, seeded and finely sliced

cilantro leaves, to garnish

shredded fresh coconut (optional)

For the dressing

2 tablespoons fish sauce

1 tablespoon brown sugar

2 tablespoons lime juice

1 Make the dressing. Whisk together the fish sauce, brown sugar and lime juice and set aside.

2 Heat the oil in a small frying pan, add the shallots and garlic and fry for 3–4 minutes, until they are golden. Remove from the pan and set aside.

3 Peel the pomelo and break the flesh into small pieces, taking care to remove any membranes.

4 Coarsely grind the peanuts, then combine with the pomelo flesh, shrimp, crab meat, mint leaves and the fried shallot mixture. Toss the salad in the dressing and serve sprinkled with the scallions, red chilies, cilantro leaves and shredded coconut, if using.

Russian Salad

Russian salad became fashionable in the hotel dining rooms of the 1920s and 1930s. Originally it consisted of lightly cooked vegetables, eggs, shellfish and mayonnaise. Today we find it diced in plastic containers at supermarket delis. This version recalls better days and plays on the theme of the Fabergé egg.

INGREDIENTS

Serves 4

16 large button mushrooms

12 ounces cooked peeled shrimp

½ cup mayonnaise

1 tablespoon lemon juice

1 large gherkin, chopped, or
    2 tablespoons capers

1 cup fava beans, shelled

8–10 small new potatoes, scrubbed
    or scraped

4 carrots, trimmed and peeled

1 cup baby corn

1 cup baby turnips, trimmed

1 tablespoon olive oil, preferably French
    or Italian

4 eggs, hard-cooked and shelled

6–8 canned anchovy fillets, cut into fine
    strips

salt and freshly ground black pepper

paprika, to garnish

1 Slice the mushrooms, then cut into matchsticks. Mix with the shrimp. Combine the mayonnaise and lemon juice and fold half into the mushrooms and shrimp, add the gherkin or capers and season.

2 Bring a large saucepan of salted water to a boil, add the fava beans and cook for 3 minutes. Drain and cool under cold running water, then pinch the beans between thumb and forefinger to release them from their tough skins. Boil the potatoes for 20 minutes and the remaining vegetables for 6 minutes. Drain and cool under running water.

3 Moisten the vegetables with olive oil and divide between 4 shallow bowls. Spoon on the dressed shrimp and place a hard-cooked egg in the center. Decorate the egg with strips of anchovy and sprinkle with paprika. Serve the remaining mayonnaise separately.

Melon and Crab Salad

A perfect summer salad when crab and melon are in generous supply.

INGREDIENTS

Serves 6

1 pound fresh cooked crab meat

½ cup mayonnaise

3 tablespoons sour cream or
   plain yogurt

2 tablespoons olive oil

2 tablespoons fresh lemon or lime juice

2–3 scallions, finely chopped

2 tablespoons finely chopped
   fresh cilantro

¼ teaspoon cayenne pepper

1½ cantaloupe or small honeydew melons

3 medium endives

salt and freshly ground black pepper

fresh cilantro sprigs, to garnish

1 Pick over the crab meat very carefully, removing any bits of shell or cartilage. Leave the pieces of crab meat as large as possible.

2 In a medium-size bowl, combine mayonnaise, sour cream or yogurt, olive oil, lemon or lime juice, scallions, chopped cilantro and cayenne pepper and season to taste with salt and pepper. Mix well, then fold the crab meat into this dressing.

3 Halve the melons and remove and discard the seeds. Cut the melons into thin slices, then remove the rind.

4 Divide the salad between 6 individual serving plates, making a decorative design with the melon slices and whole endive leaves. Place a mound of dressed crab meat on each plate and garnish the salads with one or two fresh cilantro sprigs.

Millionaire's Lobster Salad

When money is no object and you're in a decadent mood, this salad will satisfy your every whim. It is ideally served with a cool Chardonnay, Chablis or Pouilly-Fuissé wine.

INGREDIENTS

Serves 4

1 medium lobster, live or cooked

1 bay leaf

1 sprig thyme

1½ pounds new potatoes, scrubbed

2 ripe tomatoes

4 oranges

½ head chicory or radicchio

1 head Boston lettuce

¼ cup extra virgin olive oil

1 can (7 ounces) young artichokes in
   brine, quartered

salt

1 small bunch tarragon, chervil or flat
   leaf parsley, to garnish

For the dressing

2 tablespoons frozen concentrated orange
   juice, thawed

6 tablespoons (¾ stick) unsalted butter,
   diced

cayenne pepper

1 If the lobster needs to be cooked, add to a large pan of salted water with the bay leaf and thyme. Bring to a boil and simmer for 15 minutes. Cool under running water. Twist off the legs and claws, and separate the tail piece from the body section. Break the claws open with a hammer and remove the meat intact. Cut the tail piece open from the underside with a pair of kitchen shears. Slice the meat and set aside.

2 Bring the potatoes to a boil in salted water and simmer for 20 minutes. Drain, cover and keep warm. Cover the tomatoes with boiling water and set aside for 20 seconds to loosen their skins. Cool under running water and slip off the skins. Halve the tomatoes, discard the seeds, then cut the flesh into large dice.

3 To segment the oranges, remove the peel from the top, bottom and sides with a serrated knife. With a small paring knife, loosen the orange segments by cutting between the flesh and the membranes, holding the fruit over a small bowl.

4 To make the dressing, measure the thawed orange juice into a glass bowl and set it over a saucepan containing 1 inch of simmering water. Heat the juice for 1 minute, remove from the heat, then whisk in the butter, a little at a time, until the dressing reaches a coating consistency. Season to taste with salt and a pinch of cayenne pepper, cover and keep warm.

5 Wash the salad greens and spin dry. Dress with olive oil, then divide between 4 large serving plates. Moisten the potatoes, artichokes and orange segments with olive oil and distribute them among the salad greens. Lay the sliced lobster over the salad, spoon on the warm butter dressing, add the diced tomato and decorate with sprigs of fresh tarragon. Serve at room temperature.

Smoked Trout Salad

Horseradish is as good a partner to smoked trout as it is to roast beef. In this recipe it combines with yogurt to make a deliciously piquant light salad dressing.

INGREDIENTS

Serves 4

1 head oak leaf or red leaf lettuce

6–8 small tomatoes, cut into thin
    wedges

½ cucumber, peeled and thinly sliced

4 smoked trout fillets, about 7 ounces
    each, skinned and flaked

For the dressing

pinch of English mustard powder

3–4 teaspoons white wine vinegar

2 tablespoons light olive oil

scant ½ cup plain yogurt

about 2 tablespoons grated fresh or
    bottled horseradish

pinch of superfine sugar

1 First, make the dressing. Combine the mustard powder and vinegar, then gradually whisk in the oil, yogurt, horseradish and sugar. Set aside for 30 minutes.

COOK'S TIP

Salt should not be necessary in this recipe because of the saltiness of the smoked trout.

2 Place the lettuce leaves in a large bowl. Stir the dressing again, then pour half of it over the leaves and toss them lightly using two spoons.

3 Arrange the lettuce on 4 individual plates with the tomatoes, cucumber and trout. Spoon on the remaining dressing and serve immediately.

Tuna and Bean Salad

*This substantial salad makes a good
light meal and can be assembled
quickly from canned ingredients.*

INGREDIENTS

Serves 4–6

1 can (14 ounces) cannellini or borlotti
  beans

2 cans (7 ounces each) tuna, drained

¼ cup extra virgin olive oil

2 tablespoons fresh lemon juice

1 tablespoon chopped fresh parsley

3 scallions, thinly sliced

salt and freshly ground black pepper

1 Pour the beans into a large
strainer and rinse under cold
water. Drain well. Place in a
serving dish.

2 Break the tuna into fairly large
flakes and arrange over the
beans in the serving dish.

3 In a small bowl make the
dressing by combining the oil
with the lemon juice. Season with
salt and pepper and stir in the
parsley. Mix well. Pour onto the
beans and tuna.

4 Sprinkle with the sliced
scallion. Toss the salad well
before serving.

Niçoise Salad

There are probably as many versions of this salad as there are cooks in Provence. With chunks of good French bread, this regional classic makes a wonderful summer lunch or light supper.

INGREDIENTS

Serves 4–6

2 cups green beans

1 pound new potatoes, peeled and cut into
   1-inch pieces

white wine vinegar and olive oil,
   for sprinkling

1 small head romaine lettuce, washed,
   dried and torn into bite-sized pieces

4 ripe plum tomatoes, quartered

1 small cucumber, peeled, seeded
   and diced

1 green or red bell pepper, thinly sliced

4 hard-cooked eggs, shelled and quartered

24 Niçoise or black olives

1 can (8 ounces) tuna in brine, drained

1 can (2 ounces) anchovy fillets in olive
   oil, drained

basil leaves, to garnish

garlic croûtons, to serve

For the anchovy vinaigrette

4 teaspoons Dijon mustard

1 can (2 ounces) anchovy fillets in
   olive oil, drained

1 garlic clove, crushed

¼ cup lemon juice or white wine vinegar

½ cup sunflower oil

½ cup extra virgin olive oil

freshly ground black pepper

1 First, make the anchovy vinaigrette. Place the mustard, anchovy fillets and garlic in a bowl and blend together by pressing the garlic and anchovies against the sides of the bowl. Season well with pepper. Using a small whisk, blend in the lemon juice or vinegar. Slowly whisk in the sunflower oil in a thin stream and then the olive oil, whisking until the dressing is smooth and creamy.

2 Alternatively, put all the dressing ingredients except the oils in a food processor fitted with a metal blade and process. With the machine running, slowly add the oils, in a thin stream, until the vinaigrette is thick and creamy.

3 Drop the green beans into a large saucepan of boiling water and boil for 3 minutes until tender, yet crisp. Transfer the beans to a colander with a slotted spoon, then rinse under cold running water. Drain again and set aside.

4 Add the potatoes to the same boiling water, reduce the heat and simmer for 10–15 minutes, until just tender, then drain. Sprinkle with a little vinegar and olive oil and a spoonful of the anchovy vinaigrette.

5 Arrange the lettuce on a platter, top with the tomatoes, cucumber and pepper, then add the green beans and potatoes.

6 Arrange the eggs, olives, tuna and anchovies on top and garnish with the basil leaves. Drizzle the remaining anchovy vinaigrette on top of the salad and serve with garlic croûtons.

COOK'S TIP

To make garlic croûtons, slice a loaf of French bread or a larger loaf of bread into 1-inch cubes. Place the bread in a single layer on a baking sheet and bake in a preheated 350°F oven for 7–10 minutes or until golden brown, turning once. Rub the toast with a raw garlic clove and serve hot or let cool, then store in an airtight container to serve at room temperature.

Shrimp Salad with Curry Dressing

Curry spices add an unexpected twist to this salad. Warm flavors combine especially well with sweet shrimp and grated apple.

INGREDIENTS

Serves 4

1 ripe tomato

½ head iceberg lettuce, shredded

1 small onion

1 small bunch fresh cilantro

1 tablespoon lemon juice

1 pound cooked peeled shrimp

1 apple, peeled

salt

8 whole cooked shrimp, 8 lemon wedges and 4 sprigs fresh cilantro, to garnish

For the dressing

5 tablespoons mayonnaise

1 teaspoon mild curry paste

1 tablespoon ketchup

2 tablespoons water

1 To peel the tomato, pierce the skin with a knife and immerse in boiling water for 20 seconds. Drain and cool under running water. Peel off the skin. Halve the tomato, push the seeds out with your thumb and discard them. Cut the flesh into large dice.

2 Finely shred the lettuce, onion and cilantro. Add the tomato, moisten with lemon juice and season with salt.

3 To make the dressing, combine the mayonnaise, curry paste and ketchup in a small bowl. Add the water to thin the dressing and season to taste with salt.

4 Combine the shrimp with the dressing. Quarter and core the apple and grate into the mixture.

5 Distribute the shredded lettuce and onion mixture between 4 plates or bowls. Pile the shrimp mixture in the center of each and garnish with 2 whole shrimp, 2 lemon wedges and a sprig of cilantro.

COOK'S TIP

Fresh cilantro is inclined to wilt if it is not kept in water. Store it in the refrigerator, in a jar of water covered with a plastic bag, and it will stay fresh for several days.

Eggplant Salad with Dried Shrimp

An appetizing and unusual salad that you will find yourself making over and over again.

INGREDIENTS

Serves 4–6

2 eggplant

1 tablespoon oil

2 tablespoons dried shrimp, soaked and drained

1 tablespoon coarsely chopped garlic

2 tablespoons freshly squeezed lime juice

1 teaspoon brown sugar

2 tablespoons fish sauce

1 hard-cooked egg, shelled and chopped

4 shallots, finely sliced into rings

cilantro leaves and 2 red chilies, seeded and sliced, to garnish

1 Grill or roast the eggplant until charred and tender.

2 When the eggplant is cool enough to handle, peel off the skin and slice the flesh.

3 Heat the oil in a small frying pan, add the drained shrimp and garlic and fry for 3–4 minutes, until golden. Remove from the pan and set aside.

4 To make the dressing, put the lime juice, brown sugar and fish sauce in a small bowl and whisk together.

5 To serve, arrange the eggplant on a serving dish. Top with the egg, shallots and dried shrimp mixture. Drizzle on the dressing and garnish with the cilantro leaves and red chilies.

COOK'S TIP

For an interesting variation, try using salted ducks' or quails' eggs, cut in half, instead of chopped hens' eggs.

Thai Dipping Sauce

This is a delicious and traditional accompaniment to Hot Coconut Shrimp and Pawpaw Salad.

INGREDIENTS

Makes ½ cup

1 tablespoon vegetable oil

½-inch square shrimp paste, or
   1 tablespoon fish sauce

2 garlic cloves, finely sliced

¾-inch piece fresh ginger, peeled and
   finely chopped

3 small red chilies, seeded and chopped

1 tablespoon finely chopped cilantro root
   or stem

4 teaspoons sugar

3 tablespoons dark soy sauce

juice of ½ lime

1 Heat the vegetable oil in a wok, add the shrimp paste, garlic, ginger and chilies and soften without coloring, for 1–2 minutes.

2 Remove from the heat and add the cilantro, sugar, soy sauce and lime juice. The sauce will keep in a screw-top jar for up to 10 days.

Hot Coconut Shrimp and Pawpaw Salad

This exotic salad may be served with many Asian beef and chicken dishes.

INGREDIENTS

Serves 4-6

8 ounces raw or cooked shrimp, peeled
   and deveined

2 ripe pawpaws

8 ounces mixed salad greens and young
   spinach

1 firm tomato, skinned, seeded and
   roughly chopped

3 scallions, shredded

1 small bunch cilantro, shredded,
   1 large chili, sliced, and 1 turnip, carved,
   to garnish

Thai Dipping Sauce, to serve

For the dressing

1 tablespoon creamed coconut

2 tablespoons boiling water

6 tablespoons vegetable oil

juice of 1 lime

½ teaspoon hot chili sauce

2 teaspoons fish sauce (optional)

1 teaspoon sugar

1 To make the dressing, place the creamed coconut in a screw-top jar and add the boiling water to soften. Add the vegetable oil, lime juice, chili sauce, fish sauce, if using, and sugar. Shake well and set aside. Do not refrigerate.

2 If using raw shrimp, cover with cold water in a saucepan, bring to a boil and simmer for no longer than 2 minutes. Drain and set aside.

3 To prepare the pawpaws, cut each in half from top to bottom and remove the black seeds with a teaspoon. Peel off the outer skin and cut the flesh into even-size pieces. Wash the salad greens and toss in a bowl. Add the other ingredients. Pour on the dressing, garnish with the cilantro, chili and turnip, and serve with Thai Dipping Sauce.

PASTA AND RICE

Pasta with Tuna, Capers and Anchovies

This piquant sauce could be made without the addition of tomatoes—just heat the oil, add the other ingredients and heat through gently before tossing with the pasta.

Serves 4

2 cans tuna (7 ounces each) in oil

2 tablespoons olive oil

2 garlic cloves, crushed

1¾ pounds canned chopped tomatoes

6 canned anchovy fillets, drained

2 tablespoons capers in vinegar, drained

2 tablespoons chopped fresh basil

4 cups rigatoni or penne

salt and freshly ground black pepper

fresh basil sprigs, to garnish

1 Drain the oil from the tuna into a heavy saucepan, add the olive oil and heat gently until it stops "spitting."

2 Add the garlic and fry until golden. Stir in the tomatoes, lower the heat and simmer for 25 minutes, until thickened.

3 Flake the tuna and cut the anchovies in half. Stir into the sauce with the capers and chopped basil. Season well.

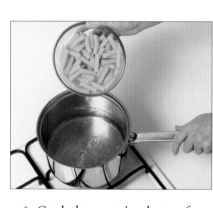

4 Cook the pasta in plenty of boiling salted water according to the manufacturer's instructions. Drain well and toss with the sauce. Garnish with fresh basil sprigs.

Farfalle with Smoked Salmon and Dill

This quick, luxurious and quite delicious sauce for pasta has now become very fashionable in Italy.

Serves 4

6 scallions, sliced

4 tablespoons (½ stick) butter

6 tablespoons dry white wine or vermouth

2 cups heavy cream

freshly grated nutmeg

8 ounces smoked salmon

2 tablespoons chopped fresh dill

freshly squeezed lemon juice

1 pound farfalle (pasta bows)

salt and freshly ground black pepper

fresh dill sprigs, to garnish

1 Slice the scallions finely. Melt the butter in a saucepan and fry the scallions for about 1 minute, until softened.

2 Add the wine and boil hard to reduce to about 2 tablespoons. Stir in the cream and add salt, pepper and nutmeg to taste. Bring to a boil and simmer for 2–3 minutes, until slightly thickened.

3 Cut the smoked salmon into 1-inch squares and stir into the sauce, together with the dill. Add a little lemon juice to taste. Keep warm.

4 Cook the pasta in plenty of boiling salted water as directed. Drain well. Toss with the sauce and serve immediately, garnished with sprigs of dill.

Tagliatelle with Smoked Salmon

This is a pretty pasta sauce that tastes as good as it looks. The light texture of the cucumber perfectly complements the fish. Different effects and color combinations can be achieved by using green, white or red tagliatelle—or even a mixture of all three.

Serves 4

12 ounces dried or fresh tagliatelle

½ cucumber

6 tablespoons (¾ stick) butter

grated rind of 1 orange

2 tablespoons chopped fresh dill

1¼ cups light cream or half-and-half

1 tablespoon orange juice

4 ounces smoked salmon, skinned

salt and freshly ground black pepper

1 If using dried pasta, cook in lightly salted boiling water following the manufacturer's instructions on the package. If using fresh pasta, cook in lightly salted boiling water for 2–3 minutes or until just tender but still firm to the bite.

2 Using a sharp knife, cut the cucumber in half lengthwise. Using a small spoon, scoop out the cucumber seeds and discard.

3 Turn the cucumber halves onto their flat sides and slice thinly.

4 Melt the butter in a heavy saucepan, add the grated orange rind and fresh dill and stir well. Add the cucumber and cook gently over low heat for about 2 minutes, stirring occasionally.

5 Add the cream, orange juice and seasoning to taste and simmer gently for 1 minute.

6 Meanwhile, cut the salmon into thin strips.

7 Stir the salmon into the sauce and heat through.

8 Drain the pasta thoroughly and toss it in the sauce. Serve immediately.

COOK'S TIP

A more economical way to make this special-occasion sauce is to use smoked salmon pieces, sold relatively inexpensively at most delicatessens and some supermarkets. (These are just scraps and awkwardly shaped pieces that are unsuitable for recipes requiring whole slices of smoked salmon.) Smoked trout is a less expensive alternative, but it lacks the rich flavor and color of smoked salmon.

Shrimp and Pasta Salad with Green Dressing

*Anchovies need a nice strong
dressing to match their flavor.*

INGREDIENTS

Serves 4-6

4 anchovy fillets, drained

¼ cup milk

8 ounces squid

1 tablespoon chopped capers

1 tablespoon chopped gherkins

1–2 garlic cloves, crushed

⅔ cup plain yogurt

2–3 tablespoons mayonnaise

squeeze of lemon juice

1 small bunch watercress, chopped finely

2 tablespoons chopped fresh parsley

2 tablespoons chopped fresh basil

12 ounces fusilli (pasta spirals)

12 ounces cooked peeled shrimp

salt and freshly ground black pepper

1 Put the anchovies into a small bowl and cover with the milk. Let soak for 10 minutes. Pull the heads off the squid and remove and discard the quills. Peel the outer speckled skin from the bodies and rinse well. Cut into ¼-inch rings. Cut the tentacles from the heads, rinse under cold water and cut into ¼-inch slices.

2 To make the dressing, mix the capers, gherkins, garlic, yogurt, mayonnaise, lemon juice and fresh herbs in a bowl. Drain and chop the anchovies. Add to the dressing with the seasoning.

3 Drop the squid rings and tentacles into a large pan of boiling salted water. Lower the heat and simmer for 1–2 minutes (do not overcook or the squid will become tough). Remove with a slotted spoon. Cook the pasta in the same water according to the instructions on the package. Drain thoroughly.

4 Mix the shrimp and squid into the dressing in a large bowl. Add the pasta, toss and serve immediately. Alternatively, let cool and serve as a salad.

Noodles with Tomatoes and Shrimps

Influences from Italy and the East combine in this dish.

Serves 4

12 ounces somen noodles

3 tablespoons olive oil

20 raw jumbo shrimp, peeled and
    deveined

2 garlic cloves, finely chopped

3–4 tablespoons sun-dried tomato paste

salt and freshly ground black pepper

For the garnish

handful of basil leaves

2 tablespoons sun-dried tomatoes in oil,
    drained and cut into strips

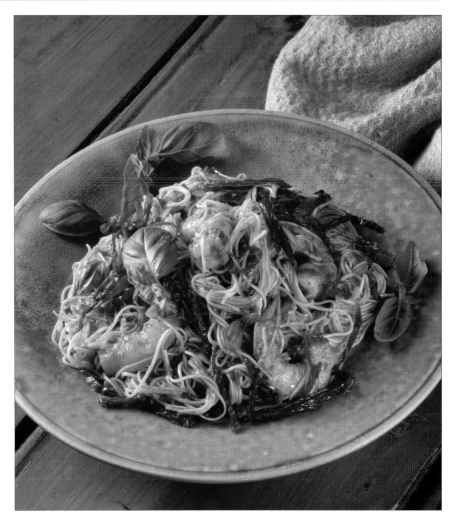

1 Cook the noodles in a large saucepan of boiling water until tender, following the directions on the package. Drain well.

2 Heat half the oil in a large frying pan. Add the shrimp and garlic and fry them over medium heat for 3–5 minutes, until the shrimp turn pink and are firm to the touch.

3 Stir in 1 tablespoon of the sun-dried tomato paste and mix well. Using a slotted spoon, transfer the shrimp to a bowl and keep hot.

4 Reheat the oil remaining in the pan. Stir in the rest of the oil with the remaining sun-dried tomato paste. You may need to add a spoonful of water if the mixture is very thick.

5 When the mixture starts to sizzle, toss in the well-drained noodles. Add salt and pepper to taste and mix well.

6 Return the shrimp to the pan and toss well to combine. Serve immediately, garnished with the basil leaves and strips of sun-dried tomatoes.

COOK'S TIP

Ready-made sun-dried tomato paste is widely available. However, you can make your own simply by processing bottled sun-dried tomatoes with their oil. You could also add a couple of anchovy fillets and some capers, if desired.

Linguine with Clams

Toss together this sauce for a real seafood flavor and serve with a light mixed salad. Canned clams make this a speedy sauce for those in a real hurry.

INGREDIENTS

Serves 4

12 ounces linguine (thin noodles)

2 tablespoons butter

2 leeks, thinly sliced

⅔ cup dry white wine

4 tomatoes, skinned, seeded and chopped

pinch of ground turmeric (optional)

1 can (9 ounces) clams, drained

2 tablespoons chopped fresh basil

¼ cup crème fraîche

salt and freshly ground black pepper

1 Cook the pasta following the instructions on the package.

2 Meanwhile, melt the butter in a small saucepan and fry the leeks for about 5 minutes until softened but not colored.

3 Add the wine, tomatoes and turmeric, if using, bring to a boil and boil until reduced by half.

4 Stir in the clams, basil, crème fraîche and seasoning to taste and heat through gently without allowing the sauce to boil.

5 Drain the pasta thoroughly and toss it in the sauce to coat. Serve immediately.

Macaroni with Jumbo Shrimp and Ham

This quick-and-easy recipe is an ideal lunch or supper dish.

INGREDIENTS

Serves 4

12 ounces macaroni

3 tablespoons olive oil

12 raw jumbo shrimp, peeled and deveined

1 garlic clove, chopped

6 ounces smoked ham, diced

⅔ cup red wine

½ small head radicchio, shredded

2 egg yolks, beaten

2 tablespoons chopped fresh flat leaf parsley

⅔ cup heavy cream

salt and freshly ground black pepper

shredded fresh basil, to garnish

1 Cook the pasta following the instructions on the package.

2 Meanwhile, heat the oil in a frying pan and cook the shrimp, garlic and ham for about 5 minutes, stirring occasionally, until the shrimp are tender.

3 Add the wine and radicchio, bring to a boil and boil rapidly until the juices are reduced by about half.

4 Stir in the egg yolks, parsley and cream and bring almost to a boil, stirring constantly, then simmer until the sauce thickens slightly. Season to taste.

5 Drain the pasta thoroughly and toss it in the sauce to coat. Serve immediately, garnished with shredded fresh basil.

COOK'S TIP

Flat leaf parsley has more flavor than the curly variety. Finely chop any leftover parsley and freeze it in a small plastic bag. It is then ready to use for cooking, but not garnishing.

Pasta with Scallops in Green Sauce

The striking colors of this dish make it irresistible.

Serves 4

½ cup low-fat crème fraîche

2 teaspoons whole-grain mustard

2 garlic cloves, crushed

2–3 tablespoons fresh lime juice

¼ cup chopped fresh parsley

2 tablespoons snipped chives

12 ounces black tagliatelle

12 large prepared scallops

¼ cup white wine

⅔ cup fish stock

salt and freshly ground black pepper

lime wedges and parsley sprigs, to garnish

1 To make the green sauce, combine the crème fraîche, mustard, garlic, lime juice, herbs and seasoning in a bowl.

2 Cook the pasta in boiling salted water according to the package instructions. Drain well.

3 Slice the scallops in half, horizontally. Keep any coral whole. Put the wine and fish stock into a saucepan. Heat to simmering point. Add the scallops and cook very gently for 3–4 minutes.

4 Remove the scallops. Boil the wine and stock vigorously to reduce by half and add the green sauce to the pan. Heat gently to warm, replace the scallops and cook for 1 minute. Spoon the sauce over the pasta and garnish with lime wedges and parsley.

Pasta with Scallops in Tomato Sauce

Delicate and simple, this pasta dish makes a good appetizer or main dish.

INGREDIENTS

Serves 4

1 pound long, thin pasta, such as fettucine
   or linguine
2 tablespoons olive oil
2 garlic cloves, finely chopped
1 pound prepared scallops, sliced in
   half horizontally
2 tablespoons chopped fresh basil
salt and freshly ground black pepper
fresh basil sprigs, to garnish

For the sauce
2 tablespoons olive oil
½ onion, finely chopped
1 garlic clove, finely chopped
2 cans (14 ounces each) peeled
   tomatoes

1 To make the sauce, heat the oil in a non-stick frying pan. Add the onion, garlic and a little salt, and cook for about 5 minutes, stirring occasionally, until just softened, but not colored.

2 Add the tomatoes with their juice, and crush with a fork. Bring to a boil, then lower the heat and simmer gently for 15 minutes. Remove the pan from the heat and set aside.

3 Bring a large pan of salted water to a boil. Add the pasta and cook until just tender to the bite, according to the instructions on the package.

4 Meanwhile, combine the oil and garlic in another non-stick frying pan and cook for about 30 seconds, until just sizzling. Add the scallops and ½ teaspoon salt and cook over high heat for about 3 minutes, tossing, until the scallops are cooked completely through.

5 Add the scallops to the tomato sauce. Season with salt and pepper to taste, then stir gently and keep warm.

6 Drain the pasta and rinse under hot water. Add the scallop sauce and the basil and toss thoroughly. Serve immediately, garnished with fresh basil sprigs.

Spaghettini with Vodka and Caviar

This is an elegant, yet easy, way to serve spaghettini. In Rome it is an after-theater favorite.

INGREDIENTS

Serves 4

¼ cup olive oil

3 scallions, thinly sliced

1 garlic clove, finely chopped

½ cup vodka

⅔ cup heavy cream

⅔ cup black or red caviar

1 pound spaghettini

salt and freshly ground black pepper

COOK'S TIP
~

The finest caviar is salted sturgeon roe. Red "caviar" is dog salmon roe, cheaper and often saltier than sturgeon roe.

---

1 Heat the oil in a small frying pan. Add the scallions and garlic, and cook gently for 4–5 minutes, until softened.

2 Add the vodka and cream, and cook over low heat for about 5–8 more minutes.

3 Remove from the heat and stir in the caviar. Season with salt and pepper, as necessary.

4 Meanwhile, cook the pasta in a large pan of rapidly boiling salted water until tender, but still firm to the bite. Drain the pasta, and toss immediately to coat with the sauce. Serve immediately.

Penne with Tuna and Mozzarella

This tasty sauce is quickly made from ingredients you are likely to have on hand, with the simple addition of fresh mozzarella and parsley. If possible, use tuna canned in olive oil.

INGREDIENTS

Serves 4

14 ounces penne, or other short pasta

1 tablespoon capers, in brine or salt

2 garlic cloves

3 tablespoons chopped fresh parsley

1 can (7 ounces) of tuna, drained

5 tablespoons olive oil

4 ounces mozzarella cheese, cut into small dice

salt and freshly ground black pepper

1 Bring a pan of salted water to the boil and cook the pasta according to package instructions.

2 Rinse the capers well in water. Chop them finely with the garlic. Combine with the parsley and the tuna. Stir in the oil, and season to taste.

3 Drain the pasta when it is just tender, but still firm to the bite. Transfer to a large frying pan. Add the tuna sauce and the diced mozzarella. Cook over medium heat, stirring constantly, until the cheese is just beginning to melt. Serve immediately.

Black Pasta with Squid Sauce

Tagliatelle flavored with squid ink looks amazing and tastes deliciously of the sea. You'll find it at good Italian delicatessens.

INGREDIENTS

Serves 4

½ cup olive oil

2 shallots, chopped

2 garlic cloves, crushed

3 tablespoons chopped fresh parsley

1½ pounds cleaned squid, cut into rings and rinsed

⅔ cup dry white wine

1 can (14 ounces) chopped tomatoes

½ teaspoon dried chili flakes or powder

1 pound black tagliatelle

salt and freshly ground black pepper

1 Heat the oil in a pan and add the shallots. Cook until pale golden in color, then add the garlic. When the garlic colors a little, add 2 tablespoons of the parsley, stir, then add the squid and stir again. Cook for 3–4 minutes, then add the wine.

2 Simmer for a few seconds, then add the tomatoes and chili flakes or powder and season with salt and pepper to taste. Cover and simmer gently for about 1 hour, until the squid is tender. Add more water if necessary.

3 Cook the pasta in plenty of boiling salted water, according to the instructions on the package, until tender, but still firm to the bite. Drain and return the pasta to the pan. Add the squid sauce and mix well. Sprinkle each serving with the remaining chopped parsley and serve immediately.

COOK'S TIP

The labeling of olive oil can be confusing. The oil is basically divided into two types—pure and virgin. The latter comes from the first pressing, but virgin olive oil is further sub-divided, according to its level of acidity. The least acidic and therefore the best oil is extra virgin. Use this quality for special dishes and salad dressings, but the next best oil—virgin— may be used for general cooking. Pure olive oil, although not in any way adulterated, lacks the unique flavor of virgin oil.

Tagliatelle with Saffron Mussels

Mussels in a saffron and cream sauce are served with tagliatelle in this recipe, but you can use any other pasta.

INGREDIENTS

Serves 4

4–4½ pounds mussels

⅔ cup dry white wine

2 shallots, chopped

12 ounces dried tagliatelle

2 tablespoons butter

2 garlic cloves, crushed

1 cup heavy cream

generous pinch of saffron strands, soaked
   in 2 tablespoons hot water

1 egg yolk

salt and freshly ground black pepper

2 tablespoons chopped fresh parsley,
   to garnish

1 Scrub the mussels under cold running water. Remove the beards. Discard any mussels with damaged shells or that do not shut immediately when sharply tapped.

2 Place the mussels in a large pan with the wine and shallots. Cover and cook over high heat, shaking the pan occasionally, for 5–8 minutes, until the mussels have opened. Drain the mussels, reserving the liquid. Discard any that remain closed. Shell all but a few of the mussels and keep warm.

3 Bring the reserved cooking liquid to a boil, then boil vigorously to reduce by about half. Strain through a fine sieve into a bowl to remove any grit.

4 Cook the tagliatelle in a pan of boiling salted water, according to the package instructions, until tender, but still firm to the bite.

5 Melt the butter in a pan and fry the garlic for 1 minute. Add the mussel liquid, cream and saffron. Heat gently, until the sauce thickens slightly. Remove from the heat and stir in the egg yolk, shelled mussels and seasoning.

6 Drain the pasta and transfer to serving bowls. Spoon on the sauce and sprinkle with chopped parsley. Garnish with the mussels in shells and serve immediately.

Sicilian Spaghetti with Sardines

A traditional dish from Sicily, with ingredients that are common to many parts of the Mediterranean.

Serves 4

12 fresh sardines, cleaned and boned

1 cup olive oil

1 onion, chopped

¼ cup fresh dill, chopped

½ cup pine nuts

½ cup raisins, soaked in water

½ cup fresh bread crumbs

1 pound spaghetti

flour for dusting

salt

1 Wash the sardines and pat them dry with paper towels. Open them out flat, then cut in half lengthwise.

2 Heat 2 tablespoons of the oil in a pan, add the onion and fry until golden. Add the dill and cook gently for 1–2 minutes. Add the pine nuts and raisins and season with salt to taste. Dry-fry the bread crumbs in a frying pan until golden. Set aside.

3 Cook the spaghetti in boiling salted water according to the instructions on the package, until tender, but still firm to the bite. Heat the remaining oil in a pan. Dust the sardines with flour and fry in the hot oil for 2–3 minutes. Drain on paper towels.

4 Drain the spaghetti and return to the pan. Add the onion mixture and toss well to coat. Transfer the spaghetti mixture to a warmed serving platter and arrange the fried sardines on top. Sprinkle with the toasted bread crumbs and serve immediately.

COOK'S TIP

Sardines are actually baby pilchards and weigh about 4 ounces. They are covered in very fine scales that are most easily removed with your hand, rather than with a scaling knife. Hold the fish by the tail under cold running water and rub your thumb and fingers gently along the body down to the head.

Smoked Haddock and Pasta in Parsley Sauce

A creamy and delicious pasta dish with a crunchy almond topping.

INGREDIENTS

Serves 4

1 pound smoked haddock fillet

1 small leek or onion, sliced thickly

1¼ cups milk

1 bouquet garni (bay leaf, thyme and parsley stalks)

2 tablespoons margarine

2 tablespoons flour

8 ounces pasta shells

2 tablespoons chopped fresh parsley

salt and freshly ground black pepper

½ cup toasted sliced almonds, to garnish

3 Put the margarine, flour and reserved milk into a pan. Bring to a boil and whisk constantly until smooth. Season, then add the fish and leek.

4 Cook the pasta in a large pan of boiling water until tender, but still firm to the bite. Drain and stir into the sauce with the chopped parsley. Serve immediately, scattered with almonds.

1 Remove all the skin and any bones from the haddock. Put into a pan with the leek, milk and bouquet garni. Bring to a boil, cover and simmer gently for 8–10 minutes, until the fish flakes easily.

2 Strain, reserving the milk for making the sauce, and discard the bouquet garni.

Baked Seafood Spaghetti

In this dish, each portion is baked and served in an individual parcel, which is then opened at the table. Use parchment paper or aluminum foil to make the parcels.

Serves 4

1 pound fresh mussels

½ cup dry white wine

¼ cup olive oil

2 garlic cloves, finely chopped

1 pound tomatoes, fresh or canned, peeled and finely chopped

14 ounces spaghetti or other long pasta

8 ounces fresh, or frozen and thawed, uncooked peeled shrimp, deveined

2 tablespoons chopped fresh parsley

salt and freshly ground black pepper

1 Scrub the mussels well under cold running water, cutting off the beards with a small sharp knife. Discard any with broken shells or that do not close immediately when sharply tapped. Place the mussels and the wine in a large saucepan and heat until they open.

2 Lift out the mussels and remove to a side dish. Discard any that do not open. Strain the cooking liquid through clean muslin to remove any grit and reserve until needed.

3 In a medium saucepan, heat the oil and garlic together for 1–2 minutes. Add the tomatoes, and cook over medium to high heat until they soften. Stir in ¾ cup of the reserved cooking liquid from the mussels and simmer gently.

4 Meanwhile, cook the pasta in a large pan of boiling salted water, according to the package instructions, until tender, but still firm to the bite.

5 Just before draining the pasta, add the shrimp and parsley to the tomato sauce. Simmer for another 2 minutes or until the shrimp are cooked through. Taste and adjust the seasoning, if necessary. Remove from the heat and set aside. Drain the pasta.

6 Prepare 4 pieces of parchment paper approximately 12 x 18 inches in size. Place each sheet in the center of a shallow bowl. Transfer the drained pasta to a mixing bowl. Add the tomato sauce and mix well. Stir in the mussels.

7 Divide the pasta and seafood between the 4 pieces of paper, placing a mound in the center of each and twisting the paper ends together to make a closed packet. (The bowl under the paper will prevent the sauce from spilling while the paper parcels are being closed.) Arrange on a large baking sheet and bake at 300°F for 8–10 minutes. Place an unopened packet on each of 4 individual serving plates.

Fusilli with Smoked Trout

The smoked trout and creamy sauce blend beautifully with the still crunchy vegetables.

INGREDIENTS

Serves 4–6

2 carrots, cut into julienne sticks

1 leek, cut into julienne sticks

2 stalks celery, cut into julienne sticks

⅔ cup vegetable stock

8 ounces smoked trout fillets, skinned and
cut into strips

8 ounces cream cheese

⅔ cup medium sweet white wine or fish
stock

1 tablespoon chopped fresh dill or fennel

8 ounces long curly fusilli

salt and freshly ground black pepper

dill sprigs, to garnish

1 Put the carrots, leek and celery into a pan with the vegetable stock. Bring to a boil and cook quickly for 4–5 minutes, until the vegetables are tender and most of the stock has evaporated. Remove from the heat and add the smoked trout.

2 To make the sauce, put the cream cheese and wine or fish stock into a saucepan, heat and whisk until smooth. Season with salt and pepper. Add the chopped dill.

3 Cook the fusilli in a large pan of boiling salted water, according to the package instructions, until tender, but firm to the bite. Drain thoroughly.

4 Return the fusilli to the pan with the sauce, toss lightly and transfer to a serving bowl. Top with the cooked vegetables and trout. Serve immediately, garnished with dill sprigs.

Spaghetti with Hot-and-sour Fish

A truly Chinese spicy taste is what makes this sauce so different.

INGREDIENTS

Serves 4

12 ounces spaghetti tricolore

1 pound monkfish, skinned

2 zucchini

1 fresh green chili, cored and seeded

1 tablespoon olive oil

1 large onion, chopped

1 teaspoon turmeric

1 cup peas, thawed if frozen

2 teaspoons lemon juice

5 tablespoons hoisin sauce

⅔ cup water

salt and freshly ground black pepper

dill sprig, to garnish

1 Cook the pasta in boiling salted water according to the instructions on the package, until tender, but still firm to the bite.

2 Meanwhile, with a large sharp knife, cut the monkfish into bite-size pieces.

COOK'S TIP

This dish is quite low in calories, so it is ideal for dieters. Hoisin sauce is widely available at most large supermarkets or Chinese food stores.

3 Thinly slice the zucchini, then finely chop the fresh, green chili. Set aside.

4 Heat the oil in a large frying pan and fry the onion for 5 minutes, until softened, but not colored. Add the turmeric.

5 Add the chili, zucchini and peas and fry over medium heat for about 5 minutes, until the vegetables have softened.

6 Stir in the fish, lemon juice, hoisin sauce and water. Bring to a boil, then simmer for about 5 minutes or until the fish is tender. Season to taste.

7 Drain the pasta thoroughly and transfer it to a serving bowl. Toss in the sauce to coat. Serve immediately, garnished with the fresh sprig of dill.

Seafood Laska

For a special occasion serve creamy rice noodles in a spicy, coconut-flavored broth, topped with a selection of seafood. There is a fair amount of work involved in the preparation, but you can make the soup base ahead.

INGREDIENTS

Serves 4

4 fresh red chilies, seeded and
    roughly chopped
1 onion, roughly chopped
1 piece balachan, the size of a stock cube
1 lemon grass stalk, chopped
1 small piece fresh ginger, roughly
    chopped
6 macadamia nuts or almonds
¼ cup vegetable oil
1 teaspoon paprika
1 teaspoon ground turmeric
2 cups stock or water
2½ cups coconut milk
fish sauce (see method)
12 raw jumbo shrimp, peeled and
    deveined
8 scallops
8 ounces prepared squid, cut into rings
12 ounces rice vermicelli or rice noodles,
    soaked in warm water until soft
salt and freshly ground black pepper
lime halves, to serve

For the garnish
¼ cucumber, cut into matchsticks
2 fresh red chilies, seeded and
    finely sliced
2 tablespoons mint leaves
2 tablespoons fried shallots

COOK'S TIP

Balachan is dried shrimp or shrimp paste. It is sold in small blocks, and you will find it at Asian supermarkets.

---

1 In a blender or food processor, process the chilies, onion, balachan, lemon grass, ginger and nuts until smooth in texture.

2 Heat 3 tablespoons of the oil in a large saucepan. Add the chili paste and fry for 6 minutes. Stir in the paprika and turmeric and fry for about 2 minutes more.

3 Add the stock and the coconut milk to the pan. Bring to a boil, reduce the heat and simmer gently for 15–20 minutes. Season to taste with the fish sauce.

4 Season the seafood with salt and pepper. Heat the remaining oil in a frying pan, add the seafood and stir-fry quickly for 2–3 minutes until cooked.

5 Add the noodles to the broth and heat through. Divide among individual serving bowls. Place the fried seafood on top, then garnish with the cucumber, chilies, mint and fried shallots. Serve with the limes.

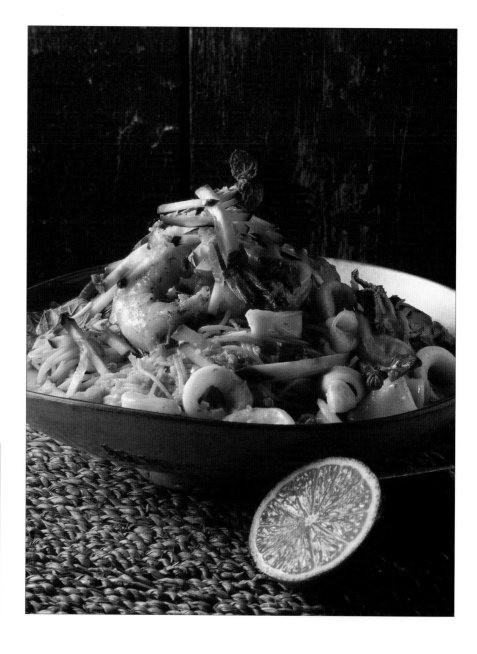

Sweet-and-sour Shrimp with Egg Noodles

A quick and easy dish full of flavor.

INGREDIENTS

Serves 4–6

½ ounce dried porcini mushrooms

1¼ cups hot water

bunch of scallions, cut into thick diagonal
  slices

1-inch piece fresh ginger, peeled and
  grated

1 red bell pepper, seeded and diced

1 can (8 ounces) water chestnuts, sliced

3 tablespoons light soy sauce

2 tablespoons sherry

12 ounces large cooked shrimp, peeled

8 ounces Chinese egg noodles

1 Put the dried porcini
mushrooms into a bowl with
the hot water and set aside to soak
for 15 minutes.

2 Put the sliced scallions,
grated ginger and diced red
pepper into a pan with the
mushrooms and their liquid. Bring
to a boil, cover and cook for about
5 minutes, until tender.

3 Add the water chestnuts, soy
sauce, sherry and shrimp.
Cover and cook gently over low
heat for 2 minutes.

4 Cook the egg noodles
according to the instructions
on the package. Drain thoroughly
and transfer to a warmed serving
dish. Spoon the hot shrimp on top.
Serve immediately.

Farfalle with Shrimp

Creamy sauces are not invariably the best way to serve fish with pasta. This simple, fresh shrimp sauce allows the distinctive flavor of the fish to be identified.

INGREDIENTS

Serves 4

8 ounces fresh or dried farfalle
   (pasta bows)
12 ounces raw or cooked shrimp
8 tablespoons (1 stick) unsalted butter
2 garlic cloves, crushed
3 tablespoons chopped fresh parsley
salt and freshly ground black pepper

1 Cook fresh pasta in boiling salted water for 2–3 minutes, or until tender but still firm to the bite. Cook dried pasta according to the package instructions. Peel and devein the shrimp.

2 Heat the butter in a large heavy saucepan with the garlic and parsley. Toss in the shrimp and sauté for 8 minutes (for cooked shrimp, 4 minutes will be sufficient).

3 Drain the pasta thoroughly and rinse with boiling water to remove any starch.

4 Stir the pasta into the shrimp mixture. Season with salt and pepper to taste and serve.

Bamie Goreng

This fried noodle dish from Indonesia is wonderfully accommodating. To the basic recipe you can add other vegetables, such as mushrooms, broccoli, leeks or bean sprouts. You can use whatever you have on hand, bearing in mind the importance of achieving a balance of colors, flavors and textures.

INGREDIENTS

Serves 6–8

1 pound dried egg noodles

1 boneless skinless chicken breast

4 ounces pork fillet

4 ounces calves' liver (optional)

2 eggs, beaten

6 tablespoons oil

2 tablespoons butter or margarine

2 garlic cloves, crushed

4 ounces cooked peeled large shrimp

4 ounces spinach

2 celery stalks, finely sliced

4 scallions, shredded

about ¼ cup chicken stock

dark soy sauce and light soy sauce

salt and freshly ground black pepper

deep-fried onions and celery leaves,
    to garnish

mixed fruit and vegetable salad, to
    serve (optional)

1 Cook the noodles in lightly salted boiling water for 3–4 minutes. Drain, rinse with cold water and drain well again. Set aside until needed.

2 Finely slice the chicken, pork fillet and calves' liver, if using.

3 Season the eggs. Heat 1 teaspoon of the oil with the butter in a small pan until melted. Stir in the eggs and keep stirring until scrambled. Set aside.

4 Heat the remaining oil in a preheated wok and stir-fry the garlic with the chicken, pork and liver for 2–3 minutes, until they have changed color. Stir in the shrimp, spinach, celery and scallions, and mix well.

5 Add the drained noodles and toss the mixture well so that all the ingredients are thoroughly combined. Add just enough stock to moisten and add dark and light soy sauce to taste. Finally, stir in the scrambled eggs.

6 Garnish the dish with deep-fried onions and celery leaves. Serve with a mixed fruit and vegetable salad, if desired.

Buckwheat Noodles with Smoked Trout

The light, crisp texture of the bok choy balances the strong, earthy flavors of the mushrooms and the smokiness of the trout.

INGREDIENTS

Serves 4

12 ounces buckwheat noodles

2 tablespoons vegetable oil

4 ounces fresh shiitake mushrooms, quartered

2 garlic cloves, finely chopped

1 tablespoon grated fresh ginger

8 ounces bok choy

1 scallion, finely sliced diagonally

1 tablespoon dark sesame oil

2 tablespoons mirin

2 tablespoons soy sauce

2 smoked trout, skinned and boned

salt and freshly ground black pepper

2 tablespoons cilantro leaves and
    2 teaspoons sesame seeds, toasted, to garnish

1 Cook the buckwheat noodles in a saucepan of boiling water for 7–10 minutes, or until just tender, according to the instructions on the package.

2 Meanwhile, heat the oil in a large frying pan. Add the shiitake mushrooms and sauté over medium heat for 3 minutes. Add the garlic, ginger and bok choy, and continue to sauté for another 2 minutes.

3 Drain the noodles and add them to the mushroom mixture, with the scallion, sesame oil, mirin and soy sauce. Toss and season with salt and pepper to taste.

4 Break up the trout into bite-size pieces. Arrange the noodle mixture on individual serving plates and top with trout.

5 Garnish the noodles with cilantro leaves and sesame seeds and serve immediately.

COOK'S TIP

Mirin is sweet, cooking sake, available at Japanese stores.

Stir-fried Noodles with Sweet Salmon

A delicious sauce forms the marinade for the salmon in this recipe. Served with soft-fried noodles, it makes a stunning dish.

INGREDIENTS

Serves 4

12 ounces salmon fillet

2 tablespoons Japanese soy sauce (shoyu)

2 tablespoons sake

¼ cup mirin or sweet sherry

1 teaspoon light brown sugar

2 teaspoons grated fresh ginger

3 cloves garlic, 1 crushed, and 2 sliced

2 tablespoons peanut oil

8 ounces dried egg noodles, cooked and drained

2 ounces alfalfa sprouts

2 tablespoons sesame seeds, lightly toasted

1 Thinly slice the salmon, then place in a shallow dish.

2 In a bowl, combine the soy sauce, sake, mirin, sugar, ginger and crushed garlic. Pour the sauce over the salmon, cover and let marinate for 30 minutes.

3 Drain the salmon, scraping off and reserving the marinade. Place the salmon in a single layer on a baking sheet. Cook under a preheated broiler for 2–3 minutes, without turning.

4 Meanwhile, heat a wok until hot, add the oil and swirl it around. Add the garlic rounds and cook until golden brown, but do not let them burn.

5 Add the cooked noodles and reserved marinade to the wok. Stir-fry for 3–4 minutes, until the marinade has reduced slightly to make a syrupy glaze that coats the egg noodles.

6 Toss in the alfalfa sprouts, then remove immediately from the heat. Transfer to warmed serving plates and top with the salmon. Sprinkle on the toasted sesame seeds. Serve immediately.

COOK'S TIP

It is important to scrape the marinade off the fish, as any remaining pieces of ginger or garlic would burn during grilling and spoil the finished dish.

Smoked Trout Cannelloni

Smoked trout can be bought already filleted or as whole fish. They make a delicious change from the tomato-based fillings usually found in cannelloni dishes.

INGREDIENTS

Serves 4-6

1 large onion, finely chopped

1 garlic clove, crushed

¼ cup vegetable stock

2 cans (14 ounces each) chopped tomatoes

½ teaspoon dried mixed herbs

1 smoked trout, about 8 ounces

¾ cup frozen peas, thawed

½ cup fresh bread crumbs

16 cannelloni tubes, cooked

salt and freshly ground black pepper

mixed salad, to serve

For the cheese sauce

2 tablespoons butter or margarine

1 tablespoon flour

1½ cups skim milk

freshly grated nutmeg

1½ tablespoons freshly grated
    Parmesan cheese

COOK'S TIP

You can use a can (7 ounces) of tuna in water instead of the trout, if preferred.

1 Simmer the onion, garlic clove and stock in a large, covered saucepan for 3 minutes. Uncover and continue to cook, stirring occasionally, until the stock has reduced entirely.

2 Stir in the tomatoes and dried herbs. Simmer uncovered for another 10 minutes or until the mixture is very thick.

3 Meanwhile, skin the smoked trout with a sharp knife. Carefully flake the flesh and discard all the bones. Combine the fish with the tomato mixture, peas, bread crumbs, salt and freshly ground black pepper.

4 Spoon the filling into the cannelloni tubes and arrange in an ovenproof dish.

5 For the sauce, put the butter, flour and milk into a saucepan and cook over medium heat, whisking constantly, until the sauce thickens. Simmer for 2–3 minutes, stirring all the time. Season to taste with salt, freshly ground black pepper and the grated nutmeg.

6 Pour the sauce over the stuffed cannelloni and sprinkle with the grated Parmesan cheese. Bake in a preheated oven at 375°F for 30–45 minutes or until the top is golden and bubbling and the sauce is cooked through. Serve with a mixed salad.

Tuna Lasagne

Lasagne does not always have to be made with ground beef.

INGREDIENTS

Serves 6

12 ounces oven-ready lasagne

1 tablespoon butter

1 small onion, finely chopped

1 garlic clove, finely chopped

4 ounces mushrooms, thinly sliced

¼ cup dry white wine (optional)

2½ cups white sauce

⅔ cup heavy cream

3 tablespoons chopped fresh parsley

2 cans (7 ounces each) tuna, drained

2 canned pimientos, cut into strips

1 cup frozen peas, thawed

4 ounces mozzarella, grated

1 ounce freshly grated Parmesan cheese

salt and freshly ground black pepper

1 Soak the sheets of lasagne in a bowl of hot water for 3–5 minutes, or prepare according to the package instructions. Drain and rinse with cold water. Lay them on a dish towel, in a single layer, to drain.

2 Melt the butter in a saucepan and gently fry the onion for 2–3 minutes, until soft but not colored. Add the garlic and mushrooms and cook until they are soft, stirring occasionally.

3 Pour in the wine, if using. Boil for 1 minute. Add the white sauce, cream and parsley and season to taste.

4 Spoon a thin layer of sauce over the base of a 12 x 9-inch baking dish. Cover with a layer of lasagne sheets. Flake the tuna. Scatter half of the tuna, pimiento strips, peas and grated mozzarella over the pasta. Spoon one-third of the remaining sauce evenly over the top and cover with another layer of lasagne sheets.

5 Repeat the layers, ending with lasagne and sauce. Sprinkle with the Parmesan. Bake in a preheated oven at 350°F for 30–40 minutes, or until bubbling hot and the top is lightly browned. Cut into squares and serve from the baking dish.

Seafood Chow Mein

*This basic recipe can be adapted
using a range of different items for
the "'dressing."*

INGREDIENTS

Serves 4

3 ounces squid, cleaned

3 ounces raw shrimp

3–4 fresh scallops, prepared

½ egg white

1 tablespoon cornstarch paste

8 ounces egg noodles

5–6 tablespoons vegetable oil

2 ounces snow peas

½ teaspoon salt

½ teaspoon light brown sugar

1 tablespoon Chinese rice wine or
 dry sherry

2 tablespoons light soy sauce

2 scallions, finely shredded

vegetable or chicken stock, if necessary

few drops sesame oil

1 Open up the squid and, using
a sharp knife, score the inside
in a crisscross pattern. Cut the
squid into pieces, each about the
size of a postage stamp. Soak the
squid in a bowl of boiling water
until all the pieces curl up. Rinse in
cold water and drain.

2 Peel and devein the shrimp,
then cut each of them in
half lengthwise.

3 Cut each scallop into 3–4 slices.
Mix the scallops and shrimp
with the egg white and cornstarch
paste and set aside.

4 Cook the noodles in boiling
water according to the package
instructions, then drain and rinse
under cold water. Mix with about
1 tablespoon of the oil.

COOK'S TIP

To make cornstarch paste, mix
4 parts dry cornstarch with about
5 parts cold water until smooth.

5 Heat 2–3 tablespoons of the
oil in a preheated wok until
hot. Stir-fry the snow peas and
seafood for about 2 minutes, then
add the salt, sugar, rice wine or
sherry, half of the soy sauce and
about half of the scallions. Blend
well and add a little stock, if
necessary. Remove and keep warm.

6 Heat the remaining oil in the
wok and stir-fry the noodles
for 2–3 minutes with the
remaining soy sauce. Place in a
large serving dish, pour the
"dressing" on top, garnish with the
remaining scallions and sprinkle
with sesame oil. Serve hot or cold.

Seafood Rice

This tasty paella-type meal uses a frozen fish mixture that saves lots of preparation time.

INGREDIENTS

Serves 4

2 tablespoons oil

1 onion, sliced

1 red bell pepper, seeded and chopped

4 ounces mushrooms, chopped

2 teaspoons ground turmeric

8 ounces arborio rice

3 cups chicken or vegetable stock

1 bag (14 ounces) frozen premium seafood selection, thawed

4 ounces frozen large tiger shrimp, thawed, peeled and deveined

salt and freshly ground black pepper

1 Heat the oil in a deep frying pan and fry the onion until it is starting to soften. Add the chopped pepper and mushrooms and fry for 1 minute.

2 Stir in the turmeric and then the rice. Stir until well mixed, then carefully pour on the stock. Season with salt and pepper, cover with a lid and let simmer gently for 15 minutes.

3 Add the seafood selection and the shrimp, stir well and turn up the heat slightly to bring the liquid back to a boil. Cover again and simmer for 15–20 more minutes, until the grains are cooked and the fish is hot. Serve the fish immediately.

COOK'S TIP

If you don't like this fish mixture, choose your own—use more shrimp and crab sticks, if you prefer, but cut down on the cooking time for the fish.

Fish with Rice

This Arabic fish dish, Sayadieh, is very popular in the Lebanon.

INGREDIENTS

Serves 4–6

juice of 1 lemon

3 tablespoons oil

2 pounds cod steaks

4 large onions, chopped

1 teaspoon ground cumin

2–3 saffron strands, soaked in
  2 tablespoons hot water

4 cups fish stock

1¼ pounds basmati or long grain rice

4 ounces pine nuts, lightly toasted

salt and freshly ground black pepper

fresh parsley, to garnish

1 Combine the lemon juice and 1 tablespoon of the oil in a shallow dish. Add the fish steaks, turning to coat, then cover and set aside to marinate for 30 minutes.

2 Heat the remaining oil in a large saucepan or flameproof casserole and fry the onions for 5–6 minutes, until softened and golden, stirring occasionally.

3 Drain the fish, reserving the marinade, and add to the pan. Fry for 1–2 minutes on each side until lightly golden, then add the cumin, saffron strands and a little salt and pepper.

4 Pour in the fish stock and the reserved marinade, bring to a boil and then simmer very gently, over low heat, for 5–10 minutes, until the fish is nearly done.

5 Transfer the fish to a plate and add the rice to the stock. Bring to a boil, then reduce the heat and simmer very gently over low heat for 15 minutes, until nearly all the stock has been absorbed.

6 Arrange the fish on the rice and cover. Steam over low heat for another 15–20 minutes.

7 Transfer the fish to a plate, then spoon the rice onto a large flat dish and arrange the fish on top. Sprinkle with lightly toasted pine nuts and garnish with fresh parsley.

COOK'S TIP

Take care when cooking the rice that the saucepan does not boil dry. Check it occasionally and add more stock or water, if it becomes necessary.

Salmon Risotto

Any rice can be used for risotto, although the creamiest ones are made with short grain arborio rice. Fresh tarragon and cucumber combine well to bring out the flavor of the salmon.

Serves 4

2 tablespoons butter

1 small bunch scallions, white part only, chopped

½ cucumber, peeled, seeded and chopped

14 ounces short grain arborio rice

4 cups chicken or fish stock

⅔ cup dry white wine

1 pound salmon fillet, skinned and diced

3 tablespoons chopped fresh tarragon

1 Heat the butter in a large saucepan and add the scallions and cucumber. Cook for 2–3 minutes without coloring.

2 Add the rice, chicken stock and wine, bring to a boil and simmer, uncovered, for 10 minutes, stirring occasionally.

3 Stir in the diced salmon and chopped tarragon. Continue cooking for another 5 minutes, then switch off the heat. Cover the pan and let stand for 5 minutes before serving.

VARIATION

Long grain rice can also be used. Choose grains that have not been precooked and reduce the stock to 3 cups per 14 ounces of rice.

Truffle and Lobster Risotto

*To capture the precious qualities of
the fresh truffle, partner it with
lobster and serve in a silky smooth
arborio. Both truffle shavings and
truffle oil are added toward the end
of cooking to preserve their flavor.*

INGREDIENTS

Serves 4

4 tablespoons (½ stick) unsalted butter

1 medium onion, chopped

14 ounces arborio or carnaroli rice

1 sprig thyme

5 cups chicken stock

⅔ cup dry white wine

1 freshly cooked lobster

3 tablespoons chopped fresh parsley
   and chervil

3–4 drops truffle oil

2 hard-cooked eggs, shelled and sliced

1 fresh black or white truffle, shaved

1 Melt the butter in a large
shallow pan, add the onion
and fry gently until soft without
letting it color. Add the rice and
thyme and stir well to coat evenly
with butter. Pour in the chicken
stock and wine, stir once and cook,
uncovered, for 15 minutes.

2 Twist off the lobster tail, cut
open the underside with
scissors and remove the white tail
meat. Slice half of the meat, then
roughly chop the remainder. Break
open the claws with a small
hammer and remove the flesh, in
one piece if possible.

3 Remove the rice from the heat,
stir in the chopped lobster
meat, herbs and truffle oil. Cover
and let stand for 5 minutes.

4 Divide among warmed dishes
and arrange the lobster and
hard-cooked egg slices and truffle
shavings on top. Serve immediately.

Rice Layered with Shrimp

This dish makes a meal in itself, requiring only pickles or raita as an accompaniment.

INGREDIENTS

Serves 4–6

2 large onions, finely sliced and deep-fried

1¼ cups plain yogurt

1½ tablespoons tomato paste

¼ cup green masala paste

1½ tablespoons lemon juice

1 teaspoon black cumin seeds

2-inch piece cinnamon stick or
   ¼ teaspoon cinnamon

4 green cardamom pods

1 pound cooked jumbo shrimp, peeled
   and deveined

8 ounces small button mushrooms

1 cup frozen peas, thawed and drained

1 pound basmati rice, soaked for
   5 minutes in boiled water and drained

1¼ cups water

1 envelope saffron powder mixed in
   6 tablespoons milk

2 tablespoons ghee or unsalted butter

salt

1 Combine the first 8 ingredients in a large bowl. Fold in the shrimp, mushrooms and peas. Let marinate for 2 hours in the refrigerator.

2 Grease the base of a heavy pan and add the shrimp, vegetables and any marinade juices. Cover with the drained rice and smooth the surface gently until you have an even layer.

3 Pour the water all over the surface of the rice. Make random holes through the rice with the handle of a spoon and pour a little saffron milk into each.

4 Place a few pats of ghee on the surface and place a circular piece of foil directly on top of the rice. Cover and cook over low heat for 45–50 minutes. Gently toss the rice, shrimp and vegetables together and serve hot.

Spicy Squid

This aromatically spiced squid dish, Cumi Cumi Smoor, is a favorite in Madura, Indonesia and is simple yet utterly delicious. Gone are the days when cleaning squid was such a chore: Now they can be bought ready-cleaned and are available at fish stores, market stalls or the freezers or fish counters of large supermarkets.

INGREDIENTS

Serves 3–4

1½ pounds squid, cleaned

3 tablespoons peanut oil

1 onion, finely chopped

2 garlic cloves, crushed

1 beefsteak tomato, skinned and chopped

1 tablespoon dark soy sauce

½ teaspoon ground nutmeg

6 cloves

⅔ cup water

juice of ½ lemon or lime

salt and freshly ground black pepper

boiled rice, to serve

1 Cut the squid bodies into ribbons and chop the tentacles. Rinse and drain well.

2 Heat a wok, toss in the squid and stir constantly for 2–3 minutes, by which time the squid will have curled into attractive shapes or firm rings. Lift out and set aside in a warm place.

3 Heat the oil in a clean pan and fry the onion and garlic, until soft and beginning to brown. Add the tomato, soy sauce, nutmeg, cloves, water and lemon or lime juice. Bring to a boil, then reduce the heat and add the squid with seasoning to taste.

4 Cook gently for another 3–5 minutes, stirring occasionally. Take care not to overcook the squid. Serve hot or warm, with boiled rice.

VARIATION

Try using 1 pound cooked peeled large shrimp in this recipe. Add them for the final 1–2 minutes.

Mackerel with Mustard and Lemon Butter

Look for bright, firm-looking, really fresh mackerel.

INGREDIENTS

Serves 4

4 fresh mackerel, about 10 ounces each, gutted and cleaned

1 bunch baby spinach

For the mustard and lemon butter

8 tablespoons (1 stick) butter, melted

2 tablespoons whole-grain mustard

grated rind of 1 lemon

2 tablespoons lemon juice

3 tablespoons chopped fresh parsley

salt and freshly ground black pepper

1 To prepare each mackerel, cut off the heads just behind the gills, using a sharp knife, then cut along the belly so that the fish can be opened out flat.

2 Place the fish on a board, skin side up, and, with the heel of your hand, press along the backbone to loosen it.

3 Turn the fish the right way up and pull the bone away from the flesh. Remove the tail and cut each fish in half lengthwise. Wash and pat dry.

4 Score the skin three or four times, then season the fish. To make the mustard and lemon butter, combine the melted butter, mustard, lemon rind and juice, parsley and seasoning. Place the mackerel on a broiler pan. Brush a little of the butter on the mackerel and broil for 5 minutes on each side, basting occasionally, until cooked through.

5 Arrange the spinach leaves in the center of 4 large plates. Place the mackerel on top. Heat the remaining butter in a small pan until sizzling and pour it over the mackerel. Serve immediately.

Turkish Cold Fish

Cold fish dishes are appreciated in the Middle East and for good reason—they are delicious. This particular version from Turkey can be made using mackerel, if preferred.

INGREDIENTS

Serves 4

¼ cup olive oil

2 pounds porgy or snapper

2 onions, sliced

1 green bell pepper, seeded and sliced

1 red bell pepper, seeded and sliced

3 garlic cloves, crushed

1 tablespoon tomato paste

¼ cup fish stock, bottled clam juice or
    water

5–6 tomatoes, skinned and sliced or 1 can
    (14 ounces) tomatoes

2 tablespoons chopped fresh parsley

2 tablespoons lemon juice

1 teaspoon paprika

15–20 green and black olives

salt and freshly ground black pepper

bread and salad, to serve

1 Heat 2 tablespoons of the oil in a large roasting pan or frying pan and fry the fish on both sides until golden brown. Remove from the pan, cover and keep warm.

2 Heat the remaining oil in the pan and fry the onion for 2–3 minutes, until softened. Add the peppers and continue cooking for 3–4 minutes, stirring occasionally, then add the garlic and stir-fry for 1 more minute.

3 Blend the tomato paste with the fish stock, clam juice or water and stir into the pan with the tomatoes, parsley, lemon juice, paprika and seasoning. Simmer very gently for 15 minutes, stirring occasionally.

4 Return the fish to the pan and cover with the sauce. Cook for 10 minutes, then add the olives and cook for another 5 minutes or until just cooked through.

5 Transfer the fish to a serving dish and pour the sauce on top. Let cool, then cover and chill until completely cold. Serve cold with bread and salad.

COOK'S TIP

One large fish looks spectacular, but it is tricky both to cook and to serve. If you prefer, buy 4 smaller fish and cook for a shorter time, until just tender and cooked through.

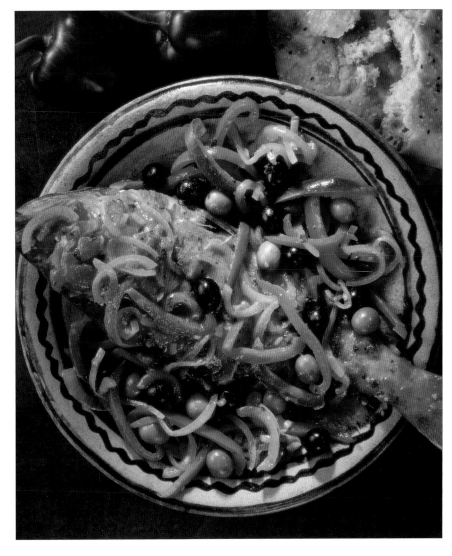

Fish Steaks with Cilantro-lime Butter

Citrus-flavored butter adds just the right kind of zip to fish steaks.

INGREDIENTS

Serves 4

1½ pounds swordfish or tuna steak,
   1 inch thick, cut into 4 pieces
¼ cup vegetable oil
2 tablespoons lemon juice
1 tablespoon lime juice
salt and freshly ground black pepper
cilantro-lime butter (see Cook's Tip)
asparagus and lime slices, to serve

1 Put the fish steaks in a shallow dish. Combine the oil, lemon juice and lime juice, season and pour over the fish. Cover and refrigerate for 1–2 hours, turning the fish once or twice.

2 Drain the fish steaks and arrange on a hot broiler pan, or set over the hot charcoal about 5 inches from the coals. Grill for 3–4 minutes or until the fish is just firm to the touch but still moist in the center, turning the steaks over once.

3 Transfer to warmed plates and top each fish steak with a pat of cilantro-lime butter. Serve the fish immediately with asparagus and slices of lime.

COOK'S TIP

For cilantro-lime butter, finely chop 1 small bunch fresh cilantro. Mix into 1 stick softened, unsalted butter, together with the grated rind and juice of 1 lime. Roll the butter neatly in waxed paper and chill in the refrigerator until firm. Other flavored butters can be made in the same way. Try parsley-lemon butter, made from 2 tablespoons chopped parsley, 1 stick unsalted butter and 1 tablespoon lemon juice.

Trout in Wine Sauce with Plantain

Tropical fish would add a distinctive flavor to this Caribbean dish.

INGREDIENTS

Serves 4

1 tablespoon garlic powder

1½ teaspoons coarse-grain black pepper

1½ teaspoons paprika

1½ teaspoons celery salt

1½ teaspoons curry powder

1 teaspoon superfine sugar

4 trout fillets

2 tablespoons butter

⅔ cup white wine

⅔ cup fish stock

2 teaspoons honey

1–2 tablespoons chopped fresh parsley

1 yellow plantain

oil, for frying

1 Combine the spices and the superfine sugar, sprinkle over the trout and marinate for 1 hour.

2 Melt the butter in a frying pan and sauté the fillets for about 5 minutes, until cooked through, turning once. Transfer to a plate and keep warm.

3 Add the wine, fish stock and honey to the pan, bring to a boil and simmer to reduce slightly. Return the fillets to the pan and spoon on the sauce. Sprinkle with parsley and simmer gently for a few minutes.

4 Meanwhile, peel the plantain, and cut into rounds. Heat a little oil in a frying pan and fry the plantain until golden, turning once. Transfer the fish to warmed serving plates, stir the sauce and pour it over the fish. Garnish with the fried plantain.

Salmon Cakes with Spicy Mayonnaise

Taste the difference between home-made fish cakes and the inferior store-bought variety with this delicious recipe.

INGREDIENTS

Serves 4

2 boiling potatoes, about 12 ounces

12 ounces salmon fillet, skinned and
    finely chopped

2–3 tablespoons chopped fresh dill

1 tablespoon lemon juice

flour, for coating

3 tablespoons vegetable oil

salt and freshly ground black pepper

spicy mayonnaise (see Cook's Tip) and
    salad greens, to serve

1 Put the potatoes in a saucepan of boiling salted water and parboil them for 15 minutes.

2 Meanwhile, combine the salmon, dill, lemon juice, salt and pepper in a large bowl.

3 Drain the potatoes and let them cool. When they are cool enough to handle, peel away the skins.

4 Shred the potatoes into strips on the coarse side of a grater.

5 Add to the salmon mixture. Combine gently with your fingers, breaking up the strips of potato as little as possible.

6 Divide the salmon and potato mixture into 8 portions. Shape each into a compact cake, pressing well together. Flatten the cakes to about ½ inch thickness.

7 Coat the salmon cakes lightly with flour, shaking off excess.

8 Heat the oil in a large frying pan. Add the salmon cakes and fry for 5 minutes or until crisp and golden brown on both sides.

9 Drain the salmon cakes on paper towels and serve with the spicy mayonnaise and salad.

COOK'S TIP

To make spicy mayonnaise, combine 1½ cups mayonnaise, 2 teaspoons Dijon mustard, ½–1 teaspoon Worcestershire sauce and a dash of Tabasco sauce. You can use home-made or good quality commercial mayonnaise.

Tuna and Corn Fish Cakes

These economical little tuna fish cakes are quick to make. Use fresh mashed potatoes or make a quick version with instant mashed potatoes.

INGREDIENTS

Serves 4

2 cups cooked mashed potatoes

1 can (7 ounces) tuna fish in soy oil, drained and flaked

¾ cup canned corn

2 tablespoons chopped fresh parsley

½ cup fresh white or brown bread crumbs

salt and freshly ground black pepper

lemon wedges, to garnish

fresh vegetables, to serve

1 Place the mashed potatoes in a bowl and stir in the tuna fish, corn and chopped parsley.

2 Season to taste with salt and pepper, then shape into 8 patty shapes with your hands.

3 Spread out the bread crumbs on a plate and gently press the fish cakes into the bread crumbs to coat lightly, then transfer to a baking sheet.

4 Cook the fish cakes under a moderately hot broiler until crisp and golden brown, turning once. Serve hot with the lemon wedges and fresh vegetables.

COOK'S TIP

For simple variations, which are just as nutritious, try using canned sardines, red or pink salmon, or smoked mackerel in place of the tuna fish.

Fresh Tuna Teriyaki

Teriyaki is a sweet soy marinade usually used to glaze meat. Here it enhances fresh tuna steaks served with rich shiitake mushrooms.

INGREDIENTS

Serves 4

4 fresh tuna or yellowfin tail steaks
   (6 ounces each)
6 ounces shiitake mushrooms, sliced
⅔ cup teriyaki sauce
8 ounces white radish, peeled
2 large carrots, peeled
salt
boiled rice, to serve

1 Season the tuna steaks with a sprinkling of salt, then set aside for 20 minutes for it to penetrate. Combine the fish and sliced mushrooms, pour the teriyaki sauce over them and set aside to marinate for another 20–30 minutes or longer if you have the time.

COOK'S TIP
~
You can make your own teriyaki sauce by combining 6 tablespoons shoyu, 1 tablespoon superfine sugar, 1 tablespoon dry white wine and 1 tablespoon rice wine or dry sherry.

2 Drain the tuna, reserving the marinade and mushrooms. Broil the tuna or grill on a barbecue for about 8 minutes, turning once.

3 Transfer the mushrooms and marinade to a stainless steel saucepan and simmer over medium heat for 3–4 minutes.

4 Slice the radish and carrots thinly, then shred finely with a chopping knife. Arrange in heaps on 4 serving plates and add the fish, with the mushrooms and sauce poured on top. Serve with plain boiled rice.

Whiting Fillets in a Polenta Crust

Polenta is sometimes called cornmeal. Use instant polenta if you can, as it will give a better crunchy coating.

INGREDIENTS

Serves 4

8 small whiting fillets

finely grated rind of 1 lemon

8 ounces polenta

2 tablespoons olive oil

1 tablespoon butter

2 tablespoons mixed fresh herbs, such as parsley, chervil and chives

salt and freshly ground black pepper

toasted pine nuts and red onion, sliced, to garnish

steamed spinach, to serve

1 Make 4 small cuts in each fillet to prevent the fish from curling up when it is cooked.

2 Sprinkle the seasoning and lemon rind over the fish.

3 Press the polenta onto the fillets. Chill in the refrigerator for 30 minutes.

4 Heat the oil and butter in a large frying pan and gently fry the fillets on each side for 3–4 minutes. Sprinkle on the fresh herbs and garnish with toasted pine nuts and red onion slices. Serve with steamed spinach.

Herrings in Oatmeal with Mustard

Oatmeal makes a delicious, crunchy coating for tender herrings.

INGREDIENTS

Serves 4

1 tablespoon Dijon mustard

1½ teaspoons tarragon vinegar

¾ cup thick mayonnaise

4 herrings, about 8 ounces each, gutted
  and cleaned

1 lemon, halved

1½ cups oatmeal

salt and freshly ground black pepper

1 Beat mustard and vinegar to taste into the mayonnaise. Chill lightly.

2 Place one fish at a time on a board, cut side down and opened out. Press gently along the backbone with your thumbs. Turn over the fish and carefully lift away the backbone.

3 Squeeze lemon juice over both sides of the fish, then season with salt and pepper. Fold the fish in half, skin side outward.

4 Place the oatmeal on a plate, then coat each herring evenly in the oatmeal, pressing it in gently but firmly.

5 Place the herrings on a broiler pan and broil for 3–4 minutes on each side, until the skin is golden brown and crisp and the flesh flakes easily. Serve immediately with the mustard sauce, served separately.

Fish and Chips

This classic British dish is quick and easy to make at home.

INGREDIENTS

Serves 4

1 cup self-rising flour

⅔ cup water

1½ pounds potatoes

oil, for deep-frying

1½-pound piece skinned cod fillet, cut
  into 4 pieces

salt

lemon wedges, to garnish

1 Sift the flour and a pinch of salt together in a bowl, then form a well in the center. Gradually pour in the water, whisking in the flour to make a smooth batter. Set aside to rest for 30 minutes.

2 Cut the potatoes into strips about ½ inch wide and 2 inches long. Place them in a colander and rinse in cold water, then drain and dry well.

3 Heat the oil in a deep-fat fryer or large heavy pan to 300°F. Using the wire basket, lower the potatoes in batches into the oil and cook for 5–6 minutes, shaking the basket occasionally, until the potatoes are soft but not browned. Remove the chips from the oil and drain thoroughly on paper towels.

4 Heat the oil in the fryer to 375°F. Season the fish. Stir the batter, then dip the pieces of fish into it, in turn, letting the excess drain off.

5 Working in two batches if necessary, lower the fish into the oil and fry for 6–8 minutes, until crisp and golden brown. Drain the fish on paper towels and keep warm.

6 Add the chips in batches to the oil and cook for 2–3 minutes, until golden brown and crisp. Keep hot. Sprinkle with salt and serve with the fish, garnished with lemon wedges.

Cod with Caper Sauce

This quick and easy sauce, with a slightly sharp and nutty flavor, is a very effective way of enhancing a rather bland fish.

INGREDIENTS

Serves 4

4 cod steaks, about 6 ounces each

8 tablespoons (1 stick) butter

1 tablespoon vinegar

1 tablespoon capers

1 tablespoon chopped fresh parsley

salt and freshly ground black pepper

tarragon sprigs, to garnish

1 Season the cod with salt and pepper. Melt 2 tablespoons of the butter, then brush some over one side of each piece of cod.

2 Cook the cod in a preheated oven for about 6 minutes, turn it over, brush with more melted butter and cook for another 5–6 minutes or until the fish flakes easily.

3 Meanwhile, heat the remaining butter until it turns golden brown, but do not let it burn. Add the vinegar, followed by the capers, and stir well.

4 Pour the vinegar, butter and capers over the fish, sprinkle with parsley and garnish with the tarragon sprigs.

COOK'S TIP
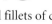
Thick tail fillets of cod or haddock could be used in place of the cod steaks, if desired.

Cod with Spiced Red Lentils

This delicious dish marries the spices of India with the delicate flavor of cod.

Serves 4

6 ounces red lentils

¼ teaspoon ground turmeric

2½ cups fish stock

2 tablespoons vegetable oil

1½ teaspoons cumin seeds

1 tablespoon grated fresh ginger

½ teaspoon cayenne pepper

1 tablespoon lemon juice

2 tablespoons chopped fresh cilantro

1 pound cod fillets, skinned and cut into
    large chunks

salt

cilantro leaves and 4–8 lemon wedges,
    to garnish

1 Put the lentils in a pan with the turmeric and stock. Bring to a boil, cover and simmer for 20–25 minutes, until the lentils are just tender. Remove from the heat and add salt to taste.

2 Heat the oil in a small frying pan. Add the cumin seeds and, when they begin to pop, add the ginger and cayenne pepper. Stir-fry the spices for a few seconds, then pour onto the lentils. Add the lemon juice and the chopped cilantro and stir in gently.

3 Lay the pieces of cod on top of the lentils, cover the pan and then cook gently over low heat for 10–15 minutes, until the fish is tender and flaky.

4 Transfer the lentils and cod to warmed serving plates. Sprinkle on the cilantro leaves and garnish each serving with 1–2 lemon wedges. Serve hot.

Fish Fillets with Orange and Tomato Sauce

Citrus flavors liven up any plain white fish beautifully.

Serves 4

3 tablespoons flour

4 fillets of firm white fish, such as cod, sea bass or sole, about 1½ pounds

1 tablespoon butter or margarine

2 tablespoons olive oil

1 onion, sliced

2 garlic cloves, chopped

¼ teaspoon ground cumin

1¼ pounds tomatoes, skinned, seeded and chopped, or 1 can (14 ounces) chopped tomatoes

½ cup fresh orange juice

salt and freshly ground black pepper

orange wedges, for garnishing

1 Put the flour on a plate and season well with salt and pepper. Coat the fish fillets lightly with the seasoned flour, shaking off any excess.

2 Heat the butter and half the oil in a large frying pan. Add the fish fillets to the pan and cook for about 3 minutes on each side, until golden brown and the flesh flakes easily when tested with a fork.

3 When the fish is cooked, transfer to a warmed serving platter. Cover with foil and keep warm while you make the sauce.

4 Heat the remaining oil in the pan. Add the onion and garlic and cook for about 5 minutes, until softened but not colored.

5 Stir in the ground cumin, tomatoes and orange juice. Bring to a boil and cook, stirring frequently, for about 10 minutes, until thickened.

6 Garnish the fish with orange wedges and serve immediately, passing the sauce separately.

Cajun-style Cod

This recipe works equally well with any firm-fleshed fish, such as swordfish, shark, tuna or halibut.

Serves 4

4 cod steaks, each weighing about
  6 ounces
2 tablespoons plain yogurt
1 tablespoon lime or lemon juice
1 garlic clove, crushed
1 teaspoon ground cumin
1 teaspoon paprika
1 teaspoon mustard powder
½ teaspoon cayenne powder
½ teaspoon dried thyme
½ teaspoon oregano
vegetable oil, for brushing
new potatoes and mixed greens,
  to serve

1 Pat the fish dry on absorbent paper towels. Combine the yogurt and lime juice and brush lightly over both sides of the fish.

2 Combine the garlic, cumin, paprika, mustard powder, cayenne, thyme and oregano. Coat both sides of the fish with the seasoning mix, rubbing in well.

3 Brush a ridged grill pan or heavy frying pan with a little oil. Heat until very hot. Add the fish and cook over high heat for 4 minutes or until the underside is well browned.

4 Brush the fish with a little more oil, if necessary, turn over and cook for another 4 minutes or until the steaks have cooked through. Serve immediately, accompanied with new potatoes and mixed greens.

Monkfish with Peppered Citrus Marinade

Monkfish is a firm, meaty fish that cooks well on the barbecue and keeps its shape.

INGREDIENTS

Serves 4

2 monkfish tails, about 12 ounces each
1 lime
1 lemon
2 oranges
handful of fresh thyme sprigs
2 tablespoons olive oil
1 tablespoon mixed peppercorns, roughly crushed
salt and freshly ground black pepper
lemon and lime wedges, to serve

3 Cut 2 slices each from the lime, lemon and 1 orange and arrange them over 2 of the fillets. Add a few sprigs of thyme and sprinkle with salt and pepper. Finely grate the rind from the remaining fruit and sprinkle it over the fish.

5 Squeeze the juice from the remaining lime, lemon and oranges and mix it with the oil and more salt and pepper to taste. Spoon over the fish. Cover and let marinate for about 1 hour, turning occasionally and spooning the marinade over it.

1 Remove any skin from the monkfish tails. Cut carefully down one side of the backbone, sliding the knife between the bone and flesh, to remove the fillet on one side. You can ask your fishmonger to do this for you.

4 Lay the remaining 2 fish fillets on top and tie them firmly with fine cotton string to hold them in shape. Arrange them in a wide dish.

6 Drain the monkfish, reserving the marinade, and sprinkle with the crushed peppercorns. Cook on a medium-hot barbecue for 15–20 minutes, basting it with the marinade and turning it occasionally, until it is evenly cooked through. Serve with lemon and lime wedges.

VARIATION

You can also use this marinade for monkfish kebabs.

2 Turn the fish and repeat on the other side, to remove the second fillet. Repeat on the second tail. Lay the 4 fillets out flat.

Haddock with Parsley Sauce

As the fish has to be kept warm while the sauce is being made, take care not to overcook it.

INGREDIENTS

Serves 4

4 haddock fillets, about 6 ounces each

4 tablespoons (½ stick) butter

⅔ cup milk

⅔ cup fish stock

1 bay leaf

4 teaspoons flour

¼ cup heavy cream

1 egg yolk

3 tablespoons chopped fresh parsley

grated rind and juice of ½ lemon

salt and freshly ground black pepper

boiled new potatoes and sliced carrots,
    to serve

1 Place the fish in a frying pan, add half the butter, the milk, fish stock, bay leaf and seasoning, and heat over medium heat to the simmering point. Lower the heat, cover the pan and poach the fish for 10–15 minutes, depending on the thickness of the fillets, until the fish is tender and the flesh just begins to flake.

2 Carefully transfer the fish to a warmed serving plate, cover and keep warm while you make the sauce. Return the cooking liquid to medium heat and bring to a boil, stirring. Simmer for about 4 minutes, then remove and discard the bay leaf.

3 Melt the remaining butter in a saucepan, stir in the flour and cook, stirring, for 1 minute. Remove from the heat and gradually stir in the fish cooking liquid. Return to the heat and bring to a boil, stirring constantly. Simmer for about 4 minutes, stirring frequently.

4 Remove the pan from the heat, blend the cream into the egg yolk, then stir into the sauce with the parsley. Reheat gently, stirring, for a few minutes.

5 Remove from the heat, add the lemon juice and rind and season to taste. Pour into a sauceboat. Serve the fish with the sauce, new potatoes and carrots.

Fish with Lemon, Red Onions and Cilantro

A rich mixture of flavors, textures and colors—and all produced in just one pan.

INGREDIENTS

Serves 4

4 halibut or cod steaks or cutlets, about
    6 ounces each
juice of 1 lemon
1 teaspoon garlic powder
1 teaspoon paprika
1 teaspoon ground cumin
¾ teaspoon dried tarragon
¼ cup olive oil
flour, for dusting
1¼ cups fish stock
2 fresh red chilies, seeded and
    finely chopped
2 tablespoons chopped fresh cilantro
1 red onion, cut into rings
salt and freshly ground black pepper

1 Place the fish in a shallow non-metallic bowl and combine the lemon juice, garlic, paprika, cumin, tarragon and a little salt and pepper. Spoon the lemon mixture over the fish, cover loosely with plastic wrap and let marinate for a few hours or overnight in the refrigerator.

2 Gently heat 3 tablespoons of the oil in a large non-stick frying pan. Dust the fish with flour, then fry for a few minutes on each side, until golden brown all over.

3 Pour the fish stock around the fish, cover and simmer for about 5 minutes, until the fish is thoroughly cooked through.

4 Add the chopped red chilies and 1 tablespoon of the cilantro to the pan. Simmer for another 5 minutes.

5 Transfer the fish and sauce to a serving plate and keep warm.

6 Meanwhile, heat the remaining olive oil and stir-fry the onion rings until speckled brown. Scatter them over the fish with the remaining chopped cilantro and serve immediately.

Marinated Fish

This dish is of Spanish origin and is also very popular throughout the Caribbean.

INGREDIENTS

Serves 4–6

1½ teaspoons garlic powder

½ teaspoon coarse-grain black pepper

½ teaspoon paprika

½ teaspoon celery salt

½ teaspoon curry powder

2 pounds cod fillet

½ lemon

1 tablespoon seasoned salt

flour, for dusting

oil, for frying

lemon wedges, to garnish

For the sauce

2 tablespoons vegetable oil

1 onion, sliced

½ red bell pepper, sliced

½ christophene or chayote, peeled and
    seeded, cut into small pieces

2 garlic cloves, crushed

½ cup malt vinegar

5 tablespoons water

½ teaspoon ground allspice

1 bay leaf

1 small hot pepper, chopped

1 tablespoon dark brown sugar

salt and freshly ground black pepper

1 Combine all the spices. Place the fish in a shallow dish, squeeze on the lemon, then sprinkle with the seasoned salt and pat into the fish. Let marinate in a cool place for 1 hour.

2 Cut the fish into 3-inch pieces and dust with a little flour, shaking off the excess.

3 Heat the oil in a heavy frying pan and fry the fish pieces for 2–3 minutes, until golden brown and crisp, turning occasionally.

4 To make the sauce, heat the oil in a heavy frying pan and fry the onion until soft. Add the pepper, christophene or chayote and garlic and stir-fry for 2 minutes. Pour in the vinegar, add the remaining ingredients and simmer gently for 5 minutes. Let stand for 10 minutes, then pour the sauce over the fish. Serve hot, garnished with lemon wedges.

Fried Fish with Piquant Mayonnaise

This sauce makes fried fish just that extra bit special and is very quick to prepare and cook, too.

Serves 4

1 egg

3 tablespoons olive oil

squeeze of lemon juice

½ teaspoon finely chopped fresh dill
   or parsley

4 whiting or haddock fillets

flour, for dusting

2 tablespoons butter or margarine

salt and freshly ground black pepper

mixed salad, to serve

For the mayonnaise

1 egg yolk

2 tablespoons Dijon mustard

2 tablespoons white wine vinegar

2 teaspoons paprika

1¼ cups olive or vegetable oil

2 tablespoons creamed horseradish

1 garlic clove, finely chopped

½ stalk celery, finely chopped

2 tablespoons ketchup

1 To make the mayonnaise, blend the egg yolk, mustard, vinegar and paprika in a mixing bowl. Add the oil in a thin stream, beating vigorously with a wire whisk to blend it in.

2 When the mixture is smooth and thick, beat in all the other mayonnaise ingredients. Cover and chill until ready to serve.

3 Combine the egg, 1 tablespoon of the olive oil, the lemon juice, the dill or parsley and a little salt and pepper in a shallow dish. Beat until well mixed.

4 Dip both sides of each fish fillet in the egg and herb mixture, then coat the fillets lightly and evenly with flour, shaking off the excess.

5 Heat the butter with the remaining olive oil in a large heavy frying pan. Fry the coated fish fillets for 8–10 minutes, until golden brown on both sides and cooked through. If necessary, cook the fish in two batches, keeping the cooked fish warm while you are cooking the remainder.

6 Serve the fish hot, with the piquant mayonnaise and accompanied by a salad.

Crumb-coated Shrimp

Serve these crunchy breaded shrimp with a homemade or store-bought dipping sauce of your choice.

INGREDIENTS

Serves 4

1½ cups polenta

about 1–2 teaspoons cayenne pepper

½ teaspoon ground cumin

1 teaspoon salt

2 tablespoons chopped fresh cilantro
    or parsley

2¼ pounds large raw shrimp, peeled
    and deveined

flour, for dredging

¼ cup vegetable oil

4 ounces coarsely grated Cheddar cheese

lime wedges and tomato salsa or relish,
    to serve

1 Mix the polenta, cayenne pepper, cumin, salt and cilantro in a bowl.

2 Coat the shrimp lightly in flour, then dip them in water and roll in the polenta mixture to coat evenly.

3 Heat the oil in a frying pan. When hot, add the shrimp, in batches if necessary. Cook for 2–3 minutes on each side, until they are cooked through. Drain on paper towels.

4 Preheat the broiler. Place the shrimp in a baking dish or in 4 individual flameproof dishes. Sprinkle on the cheese. Bake for 2–3 minutes. Serve with lime wedges and tomato salsa or relish.

Sweet-and-sour Shrimp

It is best to use raw shrimp if available. If you are using cooked ones, add them to the sauce without the initial deep-frying.

INGREDIENTS

Serves 4–6

1 pound raw jumbo shrimp in
    their shells
vegetable oil, for deep-frying
lettuce leaves, to serve

For the sauce
1 tablespoon vegetable oil
1 tablespoon finely chopped scallions
2 teaspoons finely chopped fresh
    ginger
2 tablespoons light soy sauce
2 tablespoons light brown sugar
3 tablespoons rice vinegar
1 tablespoon Chinese rice wine or
    dry sherry
about ½ cup chicken or vegetable stock
1 tablespoon cornstarch paste
few drops sesame oil

1 Pull the soft legs off the shrimp without removing the shells. Rinse and dry well with paper towels.

2 Heat the vegetable oil in a large pan or deep-fryer to 350°F and deep-fry the shrimp for 35–40 seconds or until their color changes from gray to bright orange. Remove and drain on paper towels.

3 To make the sauce, heat the oil in a preheated wok, add the scallions and ginger, followed by the seasonings and stock, and bring to a boil.

4 Add the shrimp to the sauce, blend well, then thicken the sauce with the cornstarch paste, stirring until smooth. Sprinkle with the sesame oil. Serve on a bed of lettuce.

Shrimp and Fish in an Herb Sauce

Bengalis are famous for their seafood dishes and always use mustard oil in recipes because it imparts a unique flavor and aroma. No feast is complete without one of these celebrated fish dishes.

INGREDIENTS

Serves 4–6

3 garlic cloves

2-inch piece fresh ginger

1 large leek, roughly chopped

4 green chilies

1 teaspoon vegetable oil (optional)

¼ cup mustard oil

1 tablespoon ground coriander

½ teaspoon fennel seeds

1 tablespoon crushed yellow mustard
seeds or 1 teaspoon mustard powder

¾ cup thick coconut milk

8 ounces monkfish, sliced

8 ounces raw jumbo shrimp, peeled and
deveined with tails intact

salt

1 bunch fresh cilantro leaves, chopped

green chilies, to garnish

3 Add the ground coriander, fennel seeds, mustard and coconut milk. Gently bring to a boil, then simmer, uncovered, for about 5 minutes.

4 Add the fish and simmer for 2 minutes, then fold in the shrimp and cook until the shrimp turn a bright orange-pink color. Season with salt, fold in the cilantro leaves and serve hot. Garnish with green chilies.

1 In a food processor, grind the garlic, ginger, leek and chilies into a coarse paste. Add vegetable oil if the mixture is too dry.

2 In a frying pan, heat the mustard oil with the paste until it is well blended. Keep the window open and take care not to overheat the mixture, as any smoke from the mustard oil will sting the eyes and irritate the nose.

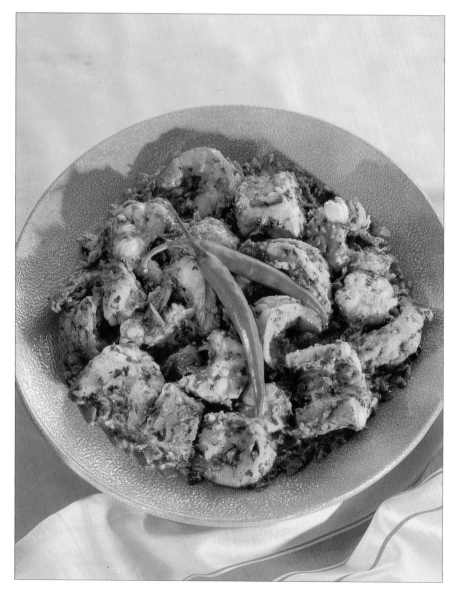

Fish and Shrimp with Spinach and Coconut

The shrimp, spinach and coconut sauce provides a truly delightful medley of flavors to complement the fish.

INGREDIENTS

Serves 4

1 pound white fish fillets, such as cod
   or haddock
1 tablespoon lemon or lime juice
½ teaspoon garlic powder
1 teaspoon ground cinnamon
½ teaspoon dried thyme
½ teaspoon paprika
seasoned flour, for dusting
vegetable oil, for shallow frying
salt and freshly ground black pepper

For the sauce
2 tablespoons butter or margarine
1 onion, finely chopped
1 garlic clove, crushed
1¼ cups coconut milk
1 small bunch fresh spinach,
   finely sliced
8–10 ounces cooked peeled shrimp
1 fresh red chili, seeded and
   finely chopped

1 Place the fish fillets in a shallow bowl and sprinkle with the lemon or lime juice.

2 Combine the garlic powder, cinnamon, thyme, paprika and salt and pepper to taste. Sprinkle the seasoning over the fish, cover loosely with plastic wrap and let marinate in a cool place or in the refrigerator for a few hours.

3 Meanwhile, make the sauce. Melt the butter in a large heavy saucepan and fry the onion and garlic for 5–6 minutes, stirring frequently, until the onion is soft.

4 Place the coconut milk and spinach in a separate saucepan and bring to a boil. Cook gently for a few minutes until the spinach has wilted and the coconut milk has reduced a little, then set aside to cool slightly.

5 Blend the spinach mixture in a blender or food processor for 30 seconds and add to the onion, together with the shrimp and red chili. Stir well and simmer gently for a few minutes, then set aside while you cook the fish.

6 Cut the fish into 2-inch pieces and dip in the seasoned flour. Heat a little oil in a large frying pan and fry the fish pieces, in batches if necessary, for 2–3 minutes on each side, until golden brown. Drain thoroughly on paper towels.

7 Arrange the fish on a warmed serving plate. Gently reheat the sauce and serve separately in a sauceboat or poured over the fish.

Braised Fish in Chili and Garlic Sauce

This recipe reflects its Chinese origins. When served in a restaurant, the fish's head and tail are usually discarded before cooking and used in other dishes. A whole fish may be used, however, and always looks impressive, especially for formal occasions and dinner parties.

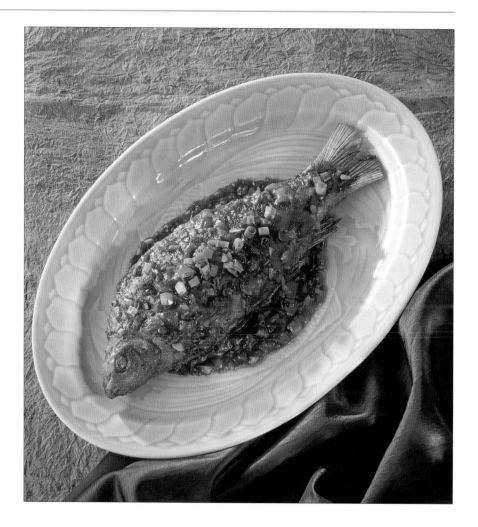

INGREDIENTS

Serves 4–6

1 carp, bream, sea bass, trout, grouper or
   striped mullet, weighing about
   1½ pounds, gutted
1 tablespoon light soy sauce
1 tablespoon Chinese rice wine or
   dry sherry
vegetable oil, for deep-frying

For the sauce

2 garlic cloves, finely chopped
2–3 scallions, finely chopped, with the
   white and green parts separated
1 teaspoon finely chopped fresh ginger
2 tablespoons hot bean sauce
1 tablespoon tomato paste
2 teaspoons light brown sugar
1 tablespoon rice vinegar
about ½ cup stock
1 tablespoon cornstarch paste
few drops sesame oil

1 Rinse and dry the fish. Score both sides of the fish, as deep as the bone, with diagonal cuts about 1 inch apart. Rub the fish with soy sauce and rice wine or sherry on both sides, then let marinate for 10–15 minutes.

2 Heat the oil in a preheated wok and deep-fry the fish for 3–4 minutes on both sides or until golden brown. Pour off the excess oil, leaving about 1 tablespoon in the wok.

3 Push the fish to one side of the wok and add the garlic, the white part of the scallions, chopped ginger, hot bean sauce, tomato paste, sugar, rice vinegar and stock. Bring to a boil and braise the fish in the sauce for 4–5 minutes, turning it over once. Add the green part of the scallions. Thicken the sauce with the cornstarch paste, sprinkle with the sesame oil, and serve immediately.

Tilapia in Fruit Sauce

Tilapia is widely used in African cooking, but can be found in most fishmongers. Yam or boiled yellow plantains are authentic—and very tasty—side dishes.

INGREDIENTS

Serves 4

4 tilapia, gutted and cleaned

½ lemon

2 garlic cloves, crushed

½ teaspoon dried thyme

2 tablespoons chopped scallions

vegetable oil, for shallow frying

flour, for dusting

2 tablespoons peanut oil

1 tablespoon butter or margarine

1 onion, finely chopped

3 tomatoes, skinned and finely chopped

1 teaspoon ground turmeric

¼ cup white wine

1 fresh green chili, seeded and
    finely chopped

2½ cups fish stock

1 teaspoon sugar

1 medium under-ripe mango, peeled,
    pitted and diced

1 tablespoon chopped fresh parsley

salt and freshly ground black pepper

1 Place the fish in a shallow bowl, squeeze lemon juice all over it and gently rub in the garlic, thyme and some salt and pepper. Place some of the scallion in the cavity of each fish, cover loosely with plastic wrap and let marinate for a few hours or overnight in the refrigerator.

2 Heat a little vegetable oil in a large frying pan, coat the fish with flour, then fry the fish on both sides for a few minutes, until golden brown. Remove from the pan to a plate, using a slotted spoon, and set aside.

3 Heat the peanut oil and butter in a saucepan and fry the onion for 4–5 minutes, until soft. Stir in the tomatoes and cook briskly for a few minutes.

4 Add the turmeric, white wine, chili, fish stock and sugar, stir well and bring to a boil, then cover and simmer gently for 10 minutes.

5 Add the fish and cook over low heat for 15–20 minutes, until the fish is cooked through. Add the mango, arranging it around the fish, and cook briefly for 1–2 minutes to heat through.

6 Arrange the fish on a warmed serving plate with the mango and tomato sauce poured on top. Garnish with chopped parsley and serve immediately.

Spanish-style Hake

Cod and haddock cutlets will also work well in this recipe.

INGREDIENTS

Serves 4

2 tablespoons olive oil

2 tablespoons butter

1 onion, chopped

3 garlic cloves, crushed

1 tablespoon flour

½ teaspoon paprika

4 hake cutlets, about 6 ounces each

8 ounces fine green beans, cut into
   1-inch lengths

1½ cups fresh fish stock

⅔ cup dry white wine

2 tablespoons dry sherry

16–20 fresh mussels, cleaned

3 tablespoons chopped fresh parsley

salt and freshly ground black pepper

crusty bread, to serve

1 Heat the oil and butter in a sauté or frying pan, add the onion and cook for 5 minutes, until softened, but not browned. Add the crushed garlic and cook for 1 more minute.

2 Combine the plain flour and paprika, then lightly dust over the hake cutlets. Push the onion and garlic to one side of the frying pan. Add the hake cutlets to the frying pan and fry until golden on both sides.

3 Stir in the beans, stock, wine, sherry and seasoning. Bring to a boil and cook for 2 minutes.

4 Add the mussels and parsley, cover and cook for 5–8 minutes, until all the mussels open. Discard any closed ones.

5 Serve in warmed shallow bowls, with crusty bread.

Halibut with Tomato Vinaigrette

Sauce vierge, an uncooked mixture of tomatoes, aromatic fresh herbs and olive oil, can either be served at room temperature or, as in this dish, tiède (slightly warm).

INGREDIENTS

Serves 4

3 large ripe beefsteak tomatoes, skinned, seeded and chopped

2 shallots or 1 small red onion, finely chopped

1 garlic clove, crushed

6 tablespoons chopped mixed fresh herbs, such as parsley, cilantro, basil, tarragon, chervil or chives

½ cup extra virgin olive oil

4 halibut fillets or steaks, 6–7 ounces each

salt and freshly ground black pepper

green salad, to serve

1 In a medium bowl, combine the tomatoes, shallots or onion, garlic and herbs. Stir in the oil and season with salt and freshly ground black pepper. Cover the bowl and set aside at room temperature for about 1 hour to let the flavors blend.

2 Preheat the broiler. Line a broiler pan with foil and brush the foil lightly with oil.

3 Season the fish with salt and pepper. Place the fish on the foil and brush with a little extra oil. Broil for 5–6 minutes, until the fish is lightly browned and cooked through.

4 Pour the sauce into a saucepan and heat gently for a few minutes. Serve the fish with the sauce and a green salad.

Seafood Balti with Vegetables

In this dish, the spicy seafood is cooked separately and combined with the vegetables at the last minute to create a truly delicious combination of flavors.

INGREDIENTS

Serves 4

8 ounces cod

8 ounces cooked peeled shrimp

6 crab sticks, halved lengthwise

1 tablespoon lemon juice

1 teaspoon ground coriander

1 teaspoon chili powder

1 teaspoon salt

1 teaspoon ground cumin

¼ cup cornstarch

⅔ cup corn oil

For the vegetables

⅔ cup corn oil

2 medium onions, chopped

1 teaspoon onion seeds

½ medium cauliflower, cut into florets

4 ounces green beans, cut into
    1-inch lengths

½ cup corn

1 teaspoon shredded fresh ginger

1 teaspoon chili powder

1 teaspoon salt

4 fresh green chilies, sliced

2 tablespoons chopped fresh cilantro

lime slices, to garnish

1 Skin the fish and cut into small cubes. Put into a medium-size mixing bowl, add the shrimp and crab sticks and set aside.

2 In a separate bowl, combine the lemon juice, ground coriander, chili powder, salt and ground cumin. Pour this over the seafood and combine thoroughly, using your hands.

3 Sprinkle on the cornstarch and mix again until the seafood is well coated. Set to one side in the refrigerator for about 1 hour to let the flavors develop.

4 To make the vegetable mixture, heat the oil in a preheated wok. Add the onions and onion seeds and stir-fry until lightly browned.

5 Add the cauliflower, green beans, corn, ginger, chili powder, salt, green chilies and fresh cilantro. Stir-fry for 7–10 minutes over medium heat.

6 Spoon the fried vegetables around the edge of a shallow dish, leaving a space in the middle for the seafood, and keep warm.

7 Wash and dry the wok or karahi, then heat the oil to fry the seafood pieces. Fry the seafood pieces in 2–3 batches, until they turn a golden brown. Remove with a slotted spoon and drain well on paper towels.

8 Arrange the batches of seafood in the middle of the dish of vegetables and keep warm while you fry the remaining seafood. Garnish with lime slices and serve.

Chunky Fish Balti with Bell Peppers

Try to find as many differently colored sweet peppers as possible to make this very attractive dish.

Serves 2–4

1 pound cod, or any other firm white fish

1½ teaspoons ground cumin

2 teaspoons mango powder

1 teaspoon ground coriander

½ teaspoon chili powder

1 teaspoon ginger pulp

3 tablespoons cornstarch

⅔ cup corn oil

3 colored bell peppers, seeded and chopped

salt

8–10 cherry tomatoes, to garnish

1 Skin the fish and cut it into small cubes. Put the fish cubes into a large mixing bowl and add the ground cumin, mango powder, ground coriander, chili powder, 1 teaspoon salt, ginger pulp and cornstarch. Combine thoroughly, using 2 spoons or your hands, until the fish is well coated.

2 Heat the oil in a preheated wok or karahi. Lower the heat and add the fish pieces, 3 or 4 at a time. Fry for about 3 minutes, turning and moving them constantly.

3 Drain the fish on paper towels. Transfer to a serving dish and keep warm while you fry the remaining fish pieces.

4 Add the peppers to the wok or karahi and fry for 2 minutes. They should still be slightly crisp. Drain on paper towels.

5 Add the drained peppers to the serving dish and garnish with the cherry tomatoes. Serve immediately.

Chinese-spiced Fish Fillets

*East meets West with this novel twist
on a classic English dish.*

INGREDIENTS

Serves 4

¾ cup flour

1 teaspoon Chinese five-spice powder

8 skinned fillets of fish, such as plaice or
   lemon sole, about 1¾ pounds total

1 egg, beaten to mix

½ cup fine fresh bread crumbs

peanut oil, for frying

2 tablespoons butter

4 scallions, cut diagonally into thin slices

2 large tomatoes, seeded and diced

2 tablespoons soy sauce

salt and freshly ground black pepper

chives and strips of red bell pepper, to
   garnish

1 Sift the flour together with the
Chinese five-spice powder and
salt and pepper to taste onto a
plate. Dip the fish fillets first in the
seasoned flour, then in beaten egg
and finally in bread crumbs.

2 Pour the oil into a large frying
pan to a depth of ½ inch. Heat
until it is very hot and starting to
sizzle. Add the coated fillets, a few
at a time, and fry for 2–3 minutes,
according to the thickness of the
fillets, until just cooked and golden
brown on both sides. Do not
crowd the pan or the temperature
of the oil will drop and the fish will
absorb too much oil.

3 Drain the fillets on paper
towels, then transfer to plates
and keep warm. Pour off all the oil
from the frying pan and wipe it
out with paper towels.

4 Melt the butter in the pan and
add the scallions and
tomatoes. Stir-fry for 1 minute.
Stir in the soy sauce.

5 Spoon the tomato mixture
over the fish and serve
immediately, garnished with the
chives and pepper strips.

Salmon with Watercress Sauce

Adding the watercress right at the end of cooking lets it retain much of its flavor and color.

INGREDIENTS

Serves 4

1¼ cups crème fraîche

2 tablespoons chopped fresh tarragon

2 tablespoons unsalted butter

1 tablespoon sunflower oil

4 salmon fillets, skinned and boned

1 garlic clove, crushed

scant ½ cup dry white wine

1 bunch watercress

salt and freshly ground black pepper

salad greens, to serve

1 Gently heat the crème fraîche in a small pan until just beginning to boil. Remove the pan from the heat and stir in half the tarragon. Let the herb cream infuse while you cook the fish.

2 Heat the butter and oil in a frying pan, add the salmon and fry for 3–5 minutes on each side. Remove from the pan and keep warm.

3 Add the garlic to the pan and fry for 1 minute, then pour in the wine and let it bubble until reduced to about 1 tablespoon.

4 Meanwhile, strip the leaves off the watercress stalks and chop finely. Discard any damaged leaves. (Save the watercress stalks for soup, if desired.)

5 Strain the herb cream into the pan and cook for a few minutes, stirring until the sauce has thickened. Stir in the remaining chopped tarragon and the watercress, then cook for a few minutes, until wilted but still bright green. Season and serve immediately, spooned over the salmon. Serve with salad greens.

Salmon with Green Peppercorns

A fashionable discovery of nouvelle cuisine, green peppercorns add piquancy to all kinds of sauces and stews. Available pickled in jars or cans, they are great to keep on hand in your pantry.

INGREDIENTS

Serves 4

1 tablespoon butter

2 or 3 shallots, finely chopped

1 tablespoon brandy (optional)

¼ cup white wine

6 tablespoons fish or chicken stock

½ cup heavy cream

2–3 tablespoons green peppercorns in brine, rinsed

1–2 tablespoons vegetable oil

4 pieces salmon fillet, 6–7 ounces each

salt and freshly ground black pepper

fresh parsley, to garnish

1 Melt the butter in a heavy saucepan over medium heat. Add the shallots and cook for 1–2 minutes, until just softened but not colored.

2 Add the brandy, if using, and the white wine, then add the stock and bring to a boil. Boil vigorously to reduce by three-quarters, stirring occasionally.

3 Reduce the heat, then add the cream and half the peppercorns, crushing them slightly with the back of a spoon. Cook very gently for 4–5 minutes, until the sauce is slightly thickened, then strain and stir in the remaining peppercorns. Keep the sauce warm over very low heat, stirring occasionally, while you cook the salmon fillets.

4 In a large heavy frying pan, heat the oil over medium-high heat until very hot. Lightly season the salmon and cook for 3–4 minutes, until the flesh is opaque throughout. To check, pierce the fish with the tip of a sharp knife; the juices should run clear. Arrange the fish on warmed plates and pour on the sauce. Garnish with parsley and serve.

Salmon with Tarragon Mushroom Sauce

Tarragon has a distinctive aniseed flavor that is good with fish, cream and mushrooms. This recipe uses oyster mushrooms to provide both texture and flavor.

INGREDIENTS

Serves 4

4 tablespoons (½ stick) unsalted butter

4 salmon steaks, 6 ounces each

1 shallot, finely chopped

6 ounces assorted wild and cultivated
   mushrooms, such as oyster
   mushrooms, trimmed and sliced

scant 1 cup chicken or vegetable stock

2 teaspoons cornstarch

½ teaspoon mustard

¼ cup crème fraîche

3 tablespoons chopped fresh tarragon

1 teaspoon white wine vinegar

salt and cayenne pepper

boiled new potatoes and green salad,
   to serve

1 Melt half the butter in a large frying pan, season the salmon and cook over medium heat for 8 minutes, turning once. Transfer to a plate, cover and keep warm.

2 Heat the remaining butter in the pan and gently fry the shallot to soften. Add the mushrooms and cook until the juices begin to flow. Add the stock and simmer for 2–3 minutes.

3 Combine the cornstarch and mustard and blend with 1 tablespoon of water. Stir into the mushroom mixture and bring to a simmer, stirring, to thicken. Add the crème fraîche, tarragon, vinegar and salt and pepper to taste.

4 Spoon the mushrooms and sauce over each salmon steak and serve with new potatoes and a green salad.

COOK'S TIP

Fresh tarragon will bruise and darken quickly after chopping, so prepare the herb just before you need it.

Grilled Butterflied Salmon

Ask your fishmonger to bone the salmon for butterflying.

INGREDIENTS

Serves 6–8

1½ tablespoons dried juniper berries

2 teaspoons dried green peppercorns

1 teaspoon superfine sugar

3 tablespoons vegetable oil

2 tablespoons lemon juice

5–5¼ pounds salmon, scaled, gutted and
    boned for butterflying

salt

lemon wedges and parsley sprigs,
    to garnish

1 Grind the juniper berries and peppercorns in a spice mill or in a mortar with a pestle. Transfer the ground spices to a small bowl and stir in the sugar, oil, lemon juice and salt to taste.

2 Open the salmon like a book, skin side down. Spread the juniper mixture evenly over the flesh. Fold the salmon closed again and place on a large plate. Cover and marinate in the refrigerator for at least 1 hour.

3 Open up the salmon again and place it, skin side down, on an oiled baking sheet. Spoon any juniper mixture left on the plate over the fish.

4 Cook under a preheated broiler, about 4 inches from the heat, for 8–10 minutes or until the fish is cooked. Serve the fish immediately, garnished with the lemon wedges and parsley.

COOK'S TIP

To bone the salmon yourself, follow the instructions for boning a round fish through the stomach. Remove both the head and tail but do not separate the fillets.

Mackerel California Style

Fish, coated with spices, are often fried until "blackened" in California, but this does make a lot of smoke in the kitchen. This recipe doesn't go quite that far.

INGREDIENTS

Serves 2–4

2 teaspoon paprika

1½ teaspoons salt

½ teaspoon onion powder

½ teaspoon garlic powder

½ teaspoon white pepper

½ teaspoon black pepper

½ teaspoon dried dill

½ teaspoon dried oregano

2 large thick mackerel, boned and filleted

8 tablespoons (1 stick) butter

lemon slices and oregano sprigs,
   to garnish

1 Combine the seasonings. Dip each fillet of mackerel into the spice mixture until well coated.

2 Heat half the butter in a large frying pan until really hot. Add the fish and cook, 2 fillets at a time, for about 2 minutes on each side. Remove immediately, add the rest of the butter and then cook the remaining fillets.

3 Serve piping hot with a little of the butter from the pan poured on top and garnished with lemon slices and sprigs of oregano.

COOK'S TIP

Other fish, such as salmon, red snapper and tuna, are also suitable, but thick cuts are best.

Trout with Curried Orange Butter

Small trout are perfect midweek fare and delicious served with this tangy butter. Children particularly like the buttery curry flavor, but it is a good idea to fillet the cooked trout and remove the bones before serving this to very young children.

INGREDIENTS

Serves 4

2 tablespoons butter, softened

1 teaspoon curry powder

1 teaspoon grated orange rind

4 small trout, gutted and heads removed

a little oil

salt and freshly ground black pepper

4 wedges of orange, to garnish

boiled new potatoes, to serve

1 Combine the butter, curry powder, orange rind and seasoning, wrap in foil and freeze for 10 minutes.

2 Brush the fish all over with oil and sprinkle well with seasoning. Make three diagonal slashes through the skin and flesh, on each side of the fish.

3 Cut the flavored butter into small pieces and insert into the slashes. Place the fish on the broiler pan and cook under a preheated broiler for 3–4 minutes on each side, depending on the thickness. Serve the fish, garnished with wedges of orange, with boiled new potatoes.

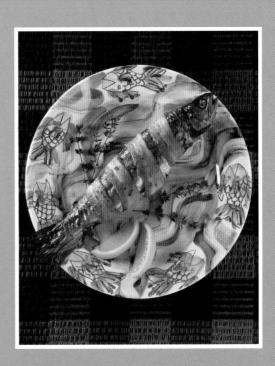

PIES AND
BAKED DISHES

~

Cod, Basil and Tomato with a Potato Crust

With a green salad, this makes an ideal dish for a substantial lunch or a family supper.

INGREDIENTS

Serves 8

2¼ pounds cod fillet

2¼ pounds smoked cod fillet

2½ cups milk

5 cups water

2 basil sprigs

1 sprig lemon thyme

6 tablespoons (¾ stick) butter

1 onion, chopped

2 tablespoons flour

2 tablespoons tomato paste

2 tablespoons chopped basil

12 medium potatoes

4 tablespoons (½ stick) butter

1¼ cups milk

salt and freshly ground black pepper

1 tablespoon chopped parsley, to serve

1 Place the cod fillet and smoked cod fillet in a roasting pan with the milk, water, basil sprigs and sprig of lemon thyme. Simmer over low heat for 3–4 minutes. Let cool in the cooking liquid for about 20 minutes. Drain the fish, reserving the liquid for use in the sauce. Flake the fish, taking care to remove any skin and bones.

2 Melt the butter in a pan, add the onion and cook for about 5 minutes, until tender but not browned. Add the flour, tomato paste and half the chopped basil. Gradually add the reserved fish cooking liquid, adding a little more milk, if necessary, to make a fairly thin sauce. Bring to the boil, season to taste with salt and pepper, and add the remaining chopped basil. Add the fish carefully and stir gently. Transfer the mixture to an ovenproof dish.

3 Boil the potatoes until tender. Add the butter and milk and mash well. Add salt and pepper to taste and spread over the fish mixture, forking to create a pattern. Bake in a preheated oven at 350°F for about 30 minutes, or until heated through. Serve with the chopped parsley.

Creamy Fish and Mushroom Pie

Fish pie is a healthy and hearty dish for a hungry family. Mushrooms go well with the fish and provide additional flavor and nourishment.

INGREDIENTS

Serves 4

8 ounces assorted wild and cultivated
   mushrooms, such as oyster, button or
   chanterelle, trimmed and quartered

1½ pounds cod or haddock fillet, skinned
   and diced

2½ cups milk, boiling

For the topping

2 pounds floury potatoes, quartered

2 tablespoons butter

⅔ cup milk

salt and freshly ground black pepper

grated nutmeg

For the sauce

4 tablespoons (½ stick) unsalted butter

1 medium onion, chopped

½ celery stalk, chopped

2 tablespoons flour

2 teaspoons lemon juice

3 tablespoons chopped fresh parsley

1   Grease an ovenproof dish, scatter the mushrooms over the base, add the fish and season with salt and pepper to taste. Pour in the boiling milk, cover the dish and cook at 400°F for 20 minutes.

2   Using a slotted spoon, transfer the fish and mushrooms to a 6-cup baking dish. Pour the poaching liquid into a bowl and reserve for use in the sauce.

3   Meanwhile, cook the potatoes in lightly salted boiling water for 20 minutes. Drain and mash with the butter and milk. Season well with salt, pepper and nutmeg.

4   To make the sauce, melt the butter in a saucepan, add the onion and celery and fry until soft, but not colored. Stir in the flour, then remove from the heat.

5   Gradually add the reserved liquid, stirring until absorbed. Return to the heat, stir and simmer to thicken. Add the lemon juice and parsley, season, then add to the baking dish.

6   Top with the mashed potatoes and return to the oven for 30–40 minutes, until the topping is golden brown.

Crunchy-topped Cod

Colorful and quick to cook, this is an ideal dish for weekday meals.

INGREDIENTS

Serves 4

4 pieces cod fillet, about 4 ounces
    each, skinned

2 medium tomatoes, sliced

½ cup fresh whole wheat bread crumbs

2 tablespoons chopped fresh parsley

finely grated rind and juice of ½ lemon

1 teaspoon sunflower oil

salt and freshly ground black pepper

mixed fresh vegetables, to serve

1 Arrange the cod fillets in a
wide ovenproof dish.

2 Arrange the tomato slices on
top. Combine the bread
crumbs, fresh parsley, lemon rind
and juice and the oil with
seasoning to taste.

3 Spoon the crumb mixture
evenly over the fish, then bake
at 400°F for 15–20 minutes. Serve
hot with mixed fresh vegetables.

Special Fish Pie

This fish pie is colorful, healthy and—best of all—very easy to make. For a more economical version, omit the shrimp and replace with more haddock fillet.

INGREDIENTS

Serves 4

12 ounces haddock fillet, skinned

2 tablespoons cornstarch

4 ounces cooked peeled shrimp

1 can (7 ounces) corn, drained

½ cup frozen peas

⅔ cup milk

4 ounces (½ package) cream cheese

¼ cup fresh whole wheat bread crumbs

1½ ounces grated Cheddar cheese

salt and freshly ground black pepper

mixed fresh vegetables, to serve

1 Cut the haddock into bite-size
pieces and toss in cornstarch to
coat evenly.

2 Place the fish, shrimp, corn
and peas in an ovenproof dish.
Beat together the milk, cream
cheese and seasonings, then pour
into the dish.

3 Combine the bread crumbs
and grated cheese, then spoon
evenly over the top of the dish.
Bake in a preheated oven at 375°F
for 25–30 minutes or until golden
brown. Serve hot with mixed
fresh vegetables.

Golden Fish Pie

Crispy, crunchy filo pastry makes a wonderful contrast to the creamy fish filling.

INGREDIENTS

Serves 4–6

1½ pounds white fish fillets

1¼ cups milk

2 slices onion

2 bay leaves

6 black peppercorns

4 ounces cooked peeled shrimp, defrosted if frozen

8 tablespoons (1 stick) butter

2 tablespoons flour

1¼ cups light cream or half-and-half

3 ounces Gruyère cheese, grated

1 bunch watercress, leaves only, chopped

1 teaspoon Dijon mustard

5 sheets filo pastry

salt and freshly ground black pepper

3 Melt 4 tablespoons (½ stick) of the butter in a pan. Stir in the flour and cook for 1 minute. Stir in the reserved cooking liquid and the cream or half-and-half. Bring to a boil, stirring continuously, then simmer for 2–3 minutes, until the sauce has thickened.

4 Remove the pan from the heat and stir in the grated Gruyère, watercress, mustard and seasoning to taste. Pour over the fish and set aside to cool.

5 Melt the remaining butter. Brush 1 sheet of filo pastry with a little melted butter, then crumple up loosely and place on top of the filling. Repeat with the remaining filo sheets and butter until they are all used up and the pie is completely covered.

6 Bake at 375°F for 25–30 minutes, or until heated through and the pastry is golden and crisp.

1 Place the fish fillets in a pan, pour in the milk and add the onion slices, bay leaves and peppercorns. Bring just to a boil, then cover and simmer for about 10–12 minutes, until the fish is almost tender.

2 Remove the fish from the pan with a slotted spoon. Skin and remove any bones, then roughly flake into a shallow ovenproof dish. Scatter the peeled shrimp over the fish. Strain the cooking liquid and reserve.

Cod with Lentils and Leeks

This unusual dish, discovered in a Parisian charcuterie, is great for entertaining. You can cook the vegetables ahead of time and let it bake while the first course is served.

INGREDIENTS

Serves 4

5 ounces green lentils

1 bay leaf

1 garlic clove, finely chopped

grated rind of 1 orange

grated rind of 1 lemon

pinch of ground cumin

1 tablespoon butter

1 pound leeks, thinly sliced or cut into julienne strips

1¼ cups whipping cream

1 tablespoon lemon juice, or to taste

1¾ pounds thick skinless cod or haddock fillets

salt and freshly ground black pepper

1 Rinse the lentils and put them in a saucepan with the bay leaf and garlic. Add enough water to cover by 2 inches. Bring to a boil and boil gently for 10 minutes, then reduce the heat and simmer for another 15–30 minutes, until the lentils are just tender.

2 Drain the lentils and discard the bay leaf, then stir in half the orange rind and all the lemon rind and season with ground cumin and salt and pepper. Transfer to a shallow baking dish or gratin dish.

3 Melt the butter in a saucepan over medium heat, then add the leeks and cook, stirring frequently, until just softened. Add 1 cup of the cream and the remaining orange rind and cook gently for 15–20 minutes. Stir in the lemon juice and season with salt and plenty of pepper.

4 Cut the fish into 4 pieces and pull out any small bones. Season the fish with salt and pepper, place on top of the lentil mixture and press down slightly into the lentils.

5 Cover each piece of fish with a quarter of the leek mixture and pour 1 tablespoon of the remaining cream over each. Bake at 375°F for about 30 minutes, until the fish is cooked through and the topping is lightly golden.

Turbot in Parchment

Cooking in parcels is not new, but it is an ideal way to cook fish. Serve this dish plain or with a little hollandaise sauce and let each person open their own parcel to savor the aroma.

Serves 4

2 carrots, cut into thin julienne strips

2 zucchini, cut into thin julienne strips

2 leeks, cut into thin julienne strips

1 fennel bulb, cut into thin julienne strips

2 tomatoes, skinned, seeded and diced

2 tablespoons chopped fresh dill, tarragon or chervil

4 turbot fillets, about 7 ounces each, cut in half

4 teaspoons olive oil

¼ cup white wine or fish stock

salt and freshly ground black pepper

1 Cut 4 pieces of non-stick baking paper, about 18 inches long. Fold each piece in half and cut into a heart shape.

2 Open the paper hearts. Arrange one-quarter of each of the vegetables next to the fold of each heart. Sprinkle with salt and pepper and half the chopped herbs. Arrange 2 pieces of turbot fillet over each bed of vegetables, overlapping the thin end of one piece and the thicker end of the other. Sprinkle the remaining herbs, the olive oil and wine or stock evenly over the fish.

3 Fold the top half of one of the paper hearts over the fish and vegetables and, beginning at the rounded end, fold the edges of the paper over, twisting and folding to form an airtight package. Repeat with the remaining three.

4 Place the parcels onto baking sheets and bake at 375°F for about 10 minutes, or until the paper is lightly browned and puffed up. Slide each parcel onto a warmed serving plate and serve immediately.

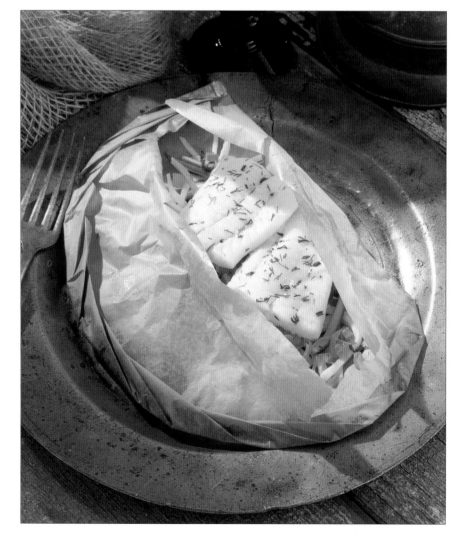

Fish Soufflé with Cheese Topping

This is an easy-going soufflé, which will not drop too much if kept waiting. On the other hand, it might be best to get the family seated before you take it out of the oven.

INGREDIENTS

Serves 4

12 ounces white fish, skinned
   and boned

⅔ cup milk

4 large cooked potatoes, still warm

1 garlic clove, crushed

2 eggs, separated

grated rind and juice of ½ small lemon

4 ounces cooked peeled shrimp

2 ounces grated Cheddar cheese

salt and freshly ground black pepper

1 Place the fish in a large saucepan and add the milk. Bring just to a boil, lower the heat and cook for 12 minutes or until it flakes easily. Alternatively, place the fish and milk in a bowl and cook in the microwave for 3–4 minutes on high. Drain, reserving the milk, and place the fish in a bowl.

2 Mash the potatoes until really creamy, using as much of the reserved fish milk as necessary. Then mash in the garlic, egg yolks, lemon rind and juice and seasoning to taste.

3 Flake the fish and gently stir into the potato mixture with the shrimp. Season to taste.

4 Whisk the egg whites until stiff, but not dry, and gently fold them into the fish mixture. When smoothly blended, spoon into a greased gratin dish.

5 Sprinkle with the cheese and bake at 425°F for 25–30 minutes, until the top is golden and just about firm to the touch. (If it browns too quickly, reduce the oven temperature to 400°F.)

Baked Red Snapper

*The flesh of the red snapper is made
tender and flavorful by rubbing in
spices and baking in a sauce.*

INGREDIENTS

Serves 3–4

1 large red snapper, gutted and cleaned
juice of 1 lemon
½ teaspoon paprika
½ teaspoon garlic powder
½ teaspoon dried thyme
½ teaspoon freshly ground black pepper
boiled rice and lemon wedges, to serve

For the sauce

2 tablespoons vegetable oil
1 onion, chopped
1 can (14 ounces) chopped tomatoes
2 garlic cloves, crushed
1 thyme sprig or ½ teaspoon dried thyme
1 fresh green chili, seeded and
    finely chopped
½ green bell pepper, seeded and chopped
1¼ cups fish stock or water

1 Prepare the sauce. Heat the
vegetable oil in a saucepan, fry
the onion for 5 minutes, then add
the chopped tomatoes, garlic,
thyme and green chili.

2 Add the pepper and stock.
Bring to a boil, stirring, then
reduce the heat, cover and simmer
for about 10 minutes, until the
vegetables are soft. Let cool a little
and then place in a blender or food
processor and blend to a purée.

3 Wash the fish well and then
score the skin with a sharp
knife in a crisscross pattern.
Combine the lemon juice, paprika,
garlic, thyme and black pepper.
Spoon the mixture over the fish
and rub in well.

4 Place the fish in a greased
baking dish and pour the
sauce on top. Cover with foil and
bake at 400°F for 30–40 minutes,
or until the fish is cooked and
flakes easily when tested with a
knife. Serve with sauce from the
dish, boiled rice and lemon wedges.

COOK'S TIP

If you prefer less sauce, remove
the foil after 20 minutes and
bake, uncovered, until cooked.

Whole Cooked Salmon

Farmed salmon has made this fish more affordable and less of a treat, but a whole salmon still makes a great centerpiece at parties. It is never served with cold meats, but is usually accompanied by salads and mayonnaise. As with all fish, the taste depends on freshness and on not overcooking it, so although you need to start the preparation early, the cooking time is short.

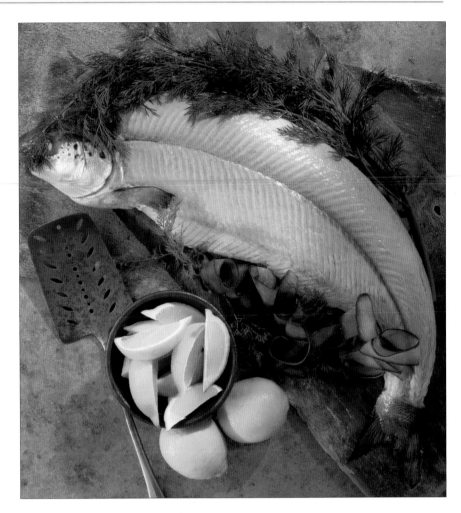

INGREDIENTS

Serves about 10 as part of a buffet

1 fresh whole salmon, 5–6 pounds

2 tablespoons oil

1 lemon

salt and freshly ground black pepper

lemon wedges, cucumber and fresh dill
   sprigs, to garnish

1 Wash the salmon and dry it well, inside and out. Pour half the oil onto a large piece of strong foil and place the fish in the center.

2 Put a few slices of lemon inside the salmon and arrange some more on the top. Season well and sprinkle on the remaining oil. Wrap up the foil to make a loose parcel. Put the parcel on another sheet of foil or a baking sheet and bake at 400°F for 10 minutes. Turn off the oven, do not open the door and let sit for several hours.

3 To serve the same day, remove the foil and peel off the skin. If you are keeping it for the following day, leave the skin on and chill the fish overnight. Arrange the fish on a large platter and garnish with lemon wedges, cucumber cut into thin ribbons and sprigs of dill.

Baked Stuffed Sardines

*Serve this nutritious dish with a
fresh tomato salad and fresh bread.*

INGREDIENTS

Serves 4

12 fresh sardines, gutted, scaled and
   heads removed
1 tablespoon sunflower oil, plus extra for
   greasing
1 onion, finely chopped
1 garlic clove, crushed
¼ cup fresh whole wheat bread crumbs
1 tablespoon whole-grain mustard
2 tablespoons chopped fresh parsley
1 egg yolk
2 tablespoons grated Parmesan cheese
grated rind and juice of 2 lemons
salt and freshly ground black pepper
lemon wedges and flat leaf parsley,
   to garnish

1 Using a sharp knife, slit the
sardines open along their
undersides, then turn each fish
over and press it firmly along the
back to loosen the backbone.
Carefully remove the backbones
and clean and dry the inside of
each sardine thoroughly.

2 Heat the oil in a saucepan and
sauté the onion and garlic
gently until softened and
beginning to brown.

3 Remove the pan from the heat
and mix in the bread crumbs,
mustard, chopped parsley, egg yolk
and Parmesan cheese. Stir in half
the lemon rind and juice and
season to taste.

4 Use the stuffing to fill the
cavities of the sardines.

5 Brush a shallow ovenproof
dish lightly with oil and add
the sardines, in a single layer. Add
the remaining lemon rind and
juice, cover with foil and bake at
375°F for 30 minutes. Garnish
with the lemon wedges and flat
leaf parsley.

COOK'S TIP

Oily fish are a good source of
vitamins A and D and are low in
saturated fat. Larger oily fish,
such as mackerel or herring,
could be substituted for the
sardines in this recipe. Allow one
fish per person.

Mediterranean Baked Fish

This informal fish dish is said to have originated with the fishermen on the Cote d'Azur, who would cook the remains of their catch for lunch in the still-warm baker's oven.

INGREDIENTS

Serves 4

3 medium potatoes

2 tablespoons olive oil, plus extra
   for drizzling

2 onions, halved and sliced

2 garlic cloves, very finely chopped

1½ pounds thick skinless fish fillets, such
   as turbot or sea bass

1 bay leaf

1 thyme sprig

3 tomatoes, skinned and thinly sliced

2 tablespoons orange juice

¼ cup dry white wine

½ teaspoon saffron threads, steeped in
   ¼ cup boiling water

salt and freshly ground black pepper

1 Cook the potatoes in boiling salted water for 15 minutes, then drain. When the potatoes are cool enough to handle, peel off the skins and slice them thinly.

COOK'S TIP

Both turbot and sea bass have a very delicate flavor, which can easily be destroyed by too rich a sauce or by overcooking.

---

2 Meanwhile, heat the oil in a heavy frying pan and fry the onions over medium-low heat for about 10 minutes, stirring frequently. Add the garlic and continue cooking for a few more minutes, until the onions are soft and golden.

3 Layer half the potato slices in an 8-cup baking dish. Cover with half the onions. Season with salt band pepper.

4 Place the fish fillets on top of the vegetables and tuck the herbs between them. Top with the tomato slices and then the remaining onions and potatoes.

5 Pour on the orange juice, wine and saffron liquid, season with salt and pepper and drizzle a little extra olive oil on top. Bake at 375°F, uncovered, for about 30 minutes, until the potatoes are tender and the fish is cooked.

Baked Cod with Garlic Mayonnaise

This unusual way of preparing cod is adapted from an Italian recipe for more typical Mediterranean fish.

INGREDIENTS

Serves 4

4 anchovy fillets

3 tablespoons chopped fresh parsley

6 tablespoons olive oil

4 cod fillets, about 1½ pounds
   total, skinned

¼ cup bread crumbs

coarsely ground black pepper

For the garlic mayonnaise

2 garlic cloves, finely chopped

1 egg yolk

1 teaspoon Dijon mustard

¾ cup vegetable oil

salt and freshly ground black pepper

1 Make the mayonnaise. First put the garlic in a mortar or small bowl and mash it to a paste. Beat in the egg yolk and mustard. Add the oil in a continuous thin stream, while beating vigorously with a small wire whisk. When the mixture is thick and smooth, season with salt and pepper. Cover the bowl and keep cool.

2 Chop the anchovy fillets very finely with the parsley. Place in a small bowl and add pepper to taste and 3 tablespoons of the oil. Stir to a paste.

3 Place the cod fillets in a single layer in an oiled baking dish. Spread the anchovy paste on the top of the cod fillets. Sprinkle with the bread crumbs and the remaining oil. Bake at 400°F for 20–25 minutes or until the bread crumbs are golden. Serve hot with the garlic mayonnaise.

Monkfish Medallions with Thyme

Monkfish has a sweet flesh that combines particularly well with Mediterranean flavors.

INGREDIENTS

Serves 4

1¼ pounds monkfish fillet, preferably in a
   single piece

3 tablespoons extra virgin olive oil

½ cup small black olives, pitted

1 large or 2 small tomatoes, seeded
   and diced

1 fresh thyme sprig or 1 teaspoon dried
   thyme leaves

salt and freshly ground black pepper

1 tablespoon very finely chopped fresh
   parsley, to garnish

1 Remove the gray membrane from the monkfish, if necessary. Cut the fish into slices ½ inch thick.

2 Heat a non-stick frying pan until it is quite hot, without oil. Sear the fish quickly on both sides. Remove and set aside.

3 Pour 1 tablespoon of the olive oil in the base of a shallow baking dish and tilt to coat. Arrange the fish in a single layer. Scatter the olives and diced tomato on top of the fish.

4 Sprinkle the fish with thyme, salt and pepper and the remaining oil. Bake at 400°F for 10–12 minutes.

5 To serve, divide the medallions between 4 warmed plates. Spoon on the vegetables and any cooking juices. Sprinkle with the chopped parsley.

Stuffed Plaice Rolls

Plaice fillets are an excellent choice for family meals because they are economical, easy to cook and free of bones—besides being delicious.

INGREDIENTS

Serves 4

2 medium carrots, grated

1 medium zucchini, grated

¼ cup fresh whole wheat bread crumbs

1 tablespoon lime or lemon juice

4 plaice fillets

salt and freshly ground black pepper

boiled new potatoes, to serve

1 Combine the grated carrots and zucchini. Stir in the bread crumbs and lime or lemon juice and season with salt and pepper.

2 Lay the fish fillets skin side up and divide the stuffing between them, spreading it evenly.

3 Roll up to enclose the stuffing and place in an ovenproof dish. Cover and bake at 400°F for about 30 minutes or until the fish flakes easily. Serve hot with boiled new potatoes.

COOK'S TIP

If desired, you can remove the skin from the plaice fillets before cooking. This recipe creates its own delicious juices, but for an extra sauce, stir chopped fresh parsley into a little sour cream and serve with the fish.

Fillets of Hake Baked with Thyme

Quick cooking is the essence of this dish. Use the freshest garlic available and, if there is no fresh thyme, use half the amount of dried thyme.

INGREDIENTS

Serves 4

4 hake fillets, 6 ounces each

1 shallot, finely chopped

2 garlic cloves, thinly sliced

4 fresh thyme sprigs

juice of 1 lemon

2 tablespoons extra virgin olive oil

salt and freshly ground black pepper

finely grated lemon rind and fresh thyme
  sprigs, to garnish

1 Arrange the hake fillets on the base of a large roasting pan. Scatter the shallot, garlic cloves and thyme on top.

2 Season well with salt and freshly ground pepper.

3 Drizzle on the lemon juice and olive oil. Bake in a preheated oven at 350°F for about 15 minutes or until the fish flakes easily. Serve, garnished with finely grated lemon rind and fresh thyme sprigs.

VARIATIONS

If hake is not available, you can use cod or haddock fillets for this recipe. You can also use a mixture of fresh herbs, such as tarragon, parsley and chervil.

COOK'S TIP

Hake is a round fish found extensively in the North and South Atlantic oceans and is extremely popular in Spain and Portugal. Its milky white flesh is delicate in flavor and quite fragile, so fillets need very careful handling, as they break up easily.

Breaded Fish with Tartar Sauce

All the taste of the classic fish dish but without any frying.

Serves 4

½ cup dried bread crumbs

1 teaspoon dried oregano

½ teaspoon cayenne pepper

1 cup milk

4 pieces of cod fillet, about 1½ pounds

3 tablespoons butter or margarine, melted

salt

For the tartar sauce

½ cup mayonnaise

½ teaspoon Dijon mustard

1–2 pickled gherkins, finely chopped

1 tablespoon drained capers, chopped

1 teaspoon chopped fresh parsley

1 teaspoon chopped fresh chives

1 teaspoon chopped fresh tarragon

salt and freshly ground black pepper

1 Grease a shallow ovenproof baking dish. Combine the bread crumbs, oregano and cayenne pepper on a plate and blend together. Mix the milk with 2 teaspoons salt in a bowl, stirring well to dissolve the salt.

2 Dip the pieces of cod fillet in the milk, then transfer to the plate and coat with the bread crumb mixture.

3 Arrange the coated fish in the prepared baking dish, in a single layer. Drizzle the melted butter over the fish.

4 Bake in the center of the oven at 450°F for 10–15 minutes, until the fish flakes easily when tested with a fork.

5 Meanwhile, combine all the ingredients for the tartar sauce in a small bowl. Stir gently to mix thoroughly. Serve the fish hot, accompanied by the tartar sauce, passed separately.

Smoked Haddock Lyonnaise

Lyonnaise dishes take their name from the city of Lyons, known for its excellent food. The term "Lyonnaise" refers to dishes prepared or garnished with onions.

INGREDIENTS

Serves 4

1 pound smoked haddock

⅔ cup milk

1 tablespoon butter

2 onions, chopped

1 tablespoon cornstarch

⅔ cup plain yogurt

1 teaspoon ground turmeric

1 teaspoon paprika

4 ounces mushrooms, sliced

2 celery stalks, chopped

2 tablespoons olive oil

12 ounces firm cooked potatoes, preferably cold, diced

1–2 ounces soft white bread crumbs

salt and freshly ground black pepper

flat leaf parsley, to garnish

2 Melt the butter and fry half the chopped onions until translucent. Stir in the cornstarch, then gradually blend in the fish cooking liquid and the yogurt and cook until thickened and smooth.

3 Stir in the turmeric, paprika, mushrooms and celery. Season to taste and add the flaked fish. Spoon into an ovenproof dish.

4 Heat the oil and fry the remaining onions until translucent. Add the diced potatoes and stir until lightly coated in oil. Sprinkle on the bread crumbs and seasoning.

5 Spoon this mixture over the fish and bake at 375°F for 20–30 minutes. Garnish with flat leaf parsley.

1 Put the smoked haddock and the milk into a large pan over low heat and poach the fish for about 15 minutes, until just cooked. Remove the haddock, reserving the cooking liquid, then flake the fish and discard the skin and any bones. Set aside.

Sand Dab Provençal

Recreate the taste of the Mediterranean with this easy-to-make fish dish.

INGREDIENTS

Serves 4

4 large sand dab fillets

2 small red onions

½ cup vegetable stock

¼ cup dry red wine

1 garlic clove, crushed

2 zucchini, sliced

1 yellow bell pepper, seeded and sliced

1 can (14 ounces) chopped tomatoes

1 tablespoon chopped fresh thyme

salt and freshly ground black pepper

potato gratin, to serve (optional)

1 Skin the sand dab fillets with a sharp knife by laying them skin side down. Holding the tail end, push the knife between the skin and flesh in a sawing movement. Hold the knife at an angle with the blade angled toward the skin.

2 Cut each onion into 8 wedges. Put into a heavy saucepan, together with the stock. Cover and simmer for 5 minutes. Uncover and continue to cook, stirring occasionally, until the stock has reduced entirely. Add the wine and garlic clove to the pan and continue to cook until the onions are soft.

3 Add the zucchini, yellow pepper, tomatoes and thyme and season with salt and pepper to taste. Simmer for 3 minutes. Spoon the sauce into a large casserole.

4 Fold each fillet in half and place on top of the sauce. Cover and bake at 350°F for 15–20 minutes, until the fish is opaque and cooked. Serve immediately with potato gratin, if desired.

Stuffed Swordfish Rolls

Swordfish is abundant in the waters around Sicily and is featured in many dishes there.

Serves 4

4 slices fresh swordfish, about ½ inch thick

6 tablespoons olive oil

1 garlic clove, finely chopped (optional)

¼ cup bread crumbs

2 tablespoons capers, rinsed, drained
   and chopped

10 leaves fresh basil, chopped

¼ cup fresh lemon juice

salt and freshly ground black pepper

For the tomato sauce

2 tablespoons olive oil

1 garlic clove, crushed

1 small onion, finely chopped

1 pound tomatoes, skinned

½ cup dry white wine

salt and freshly ground black pepper

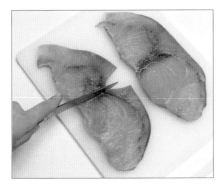

1 Cut the swordfish slices in half, removing any bones. Brush with 2 tablespoons of the olive oil, and refrigerate until needed.

2 Make the tomato sauce by heating the oil in a medium-size heavy saucepan. Add the garlic, and cook until golden. Discard the garlic. Add the onion, and cook over low heat until soft. Stir in the tomatoes and wine. Season with salt and pepper. Cover the pan, and cook over medium heat for 15 minutes.

3 Pass the sauce through a food mill or purée in a food processor. Keep warm while you prepare the fish.

4 In a small bowl combine 2 tablespoons of olive oil with the garlic, if using, bread crumbs, capers, basil and lemon juice. Season with salt and pepper and mix to a paste.

5 Lay the swordfish slices flat on a cutting board. Divide the stuffing mixture equally between the slices and spread it evenly over the center of each. Roll up the swordfish slices and secure with wooden toothpicks.

6 Heat the remaining oil in a flameproof dish. Add the swordfish rolls and brown them for 3–4 minutes over high heat, turning them once or twice. Pour in the tomato sauce and bake at 400°F for 15 minutes, basting occasionally. Serve warm.

Indian Fish Stew

*A spicy fish stew made with
potatoes, peppers and traditional
Indian spices.*

INGREDIENTS

Serves 4

2 tablespoons oil

1 teaspoon cumin seeds

1 onion, chopped

1 red bell pepper, thinly sliced

1 garlic clove, crushed

2 red chilies, finely chopped

2 bay leaves

½ teaspoon salt

1 teaspoon ground cumin

1 teaspoon ground coriander

1 teaspoon chili powder

1 can (14 ounces) chopped tomatoes

2 large potatoes, cut into 1-inch chunks

1¼ cups fish stock

4 cod fillets

chappatis, to serve

1 Heat the oil in a large deep-sided frying pan and fry the cumin seeds for 2 minutes, until they begin to splutter. Add the onion, pepper, garlic, chilies and bay leaves and fry for 5–7 minutes, until the onions have browned.

2 Add the salt, ground cumin, ground coriander and chili powder and cook for 3–4 minutes.

3 Stir in the chopped tomatoes, potatoes and fish stock. Bring to a boil and simmer for another 10 minutes.

4 Add the fish, then cover and simmer for 10 minutes or until the fish is tender. Serve with freshly cooked chappatis.

Tanzanian Fish Curry

A deliciously fragrant sauce full of tender fish.

INGREDIENTS

Serves 2–3

1 large snapper or red bream

1 lemon

3 tablespoons vegetable oil

1 onion, finely chopped

2 garlic cloves, crushed

3 tablespoons curry powder

1 can (14 ounces) chopped tomatoes

4 teaspoons smooth unsalted peanut
    butter

½ green bell pepper, chopped

2 slices fresh ginger

1 fresh green chili, seeded and
    finely chopped

2½ cups fish stock

1 tablespoon finely chopped fresh cilantro

salt and freshly ground black pepper

1 Season the fish, inside and out, with salt and pepper and place in a shallow bowl. Halve the lemon and squeeze the juice all over the fish. Cover loosely with plastic wrap and set aside to marinate for at least 2 hours.

2 Heat the oil in a large saucepan and fry the onion and garlic for 5–6 minutes, until soft. Reduce the heat, add the curry powder and cook, stirring constantly, for another 5 minutes.

3 Stir in the tomatoes and then the peanut butter, mixing well. Then add the green bell pepper, ginger, chili and stock. Stir well and simmer gently for 10 minutes.

4 Cut the fish into pieces and gently lower into the sauce. Simmer for another 20 minutes or until the fish is cooked. Using a slotted spoon, transfer the fish pieces to a plate.

5 Stir the cilantro into the sauce and adjust the seasoning. If the sauce is very thick, add a little extra stock or water. Return the fish to the sauce, cook gently to heat through and then serve immediately.

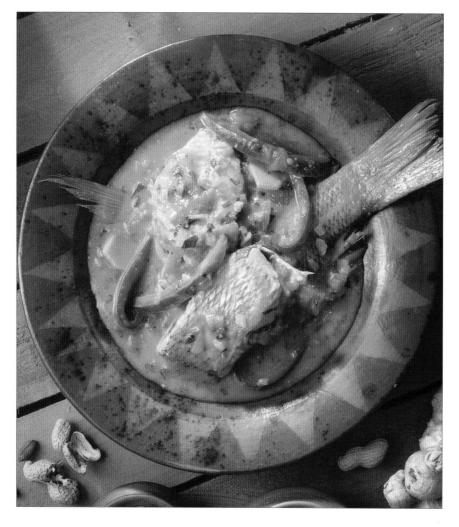

COOK'S TIP

The fish can be fried before it is added to the sauce, if preferred. Dip it in seasoned flour and fry in oil in a large frying pan or a wok for a few minutes before adding to the sauce.

Crab and Corn Gumbo

Gumbos are traditional Creole dishes, which come from New Orleans, Louisiana, and always contain a roux that gives this dish a distinctly rich flavor.

INGREDIENTS

Serves 4

2 tablespoons butter or margarine

2 tablespoons flour

1 tablespoon vegetable oil

1 onion, finely chopped

4 ounces okra, trimmed and chopped

2 garlic cloves, crushed

1 tablespoon finely chopped celery

2½ cups fish stock

⅔ cup sherry

1 tablespoon ketchup

½ teaspoon dried oregano

¼ teaspoon pumpkin pie spice

2 teaspoons Worcestershire sauce

2 corn cobs, sliced

1 pound crab claws

cayenne pepper

fresh cilantro sprigs, to garnish

1 Melt the butter or margarine in a large saucepan over a low heat, add the flour and stir together to make a roux. Cook for about 10 minutes, stirring constantly to prevent burning, while the roux turns golden brown and then darkens to a rich, nutty brown. If black specks appear, the roux must be discarded. Turn the roux onto a plate and set aside.

2 Heat the oil in the same saucepan over medium heat, add the onion, okra, garlic and celery and stir to combine. Cook for a few minutes, then add the fish stock, sherry, ketchup, oregano, pumpkin pie spice, Worcestershire sauce and cayenne pepper to taste.

3 Bring to a boil, then simmer gently for about 10 minutes, until the vegetables are tender. Add the roux, stirring it well into the sauce, and cook for a few minutes, until thickened.

4 Add the corn cobs and crab claws and continue to simmer gently over low heat for about 10 minutes, until the crab and corn are cooked.

5 Spoon onto warmed serving plates and garnish with sprigs of fresh cilantro.

Fisherman's Stew

A chunky, hearty stew that is warming in winter. The stock used here is especially aromatic, but if you do not have time to prepare it, use a basic fish stock instead.

INGREDIENTS

Serves 4

6 strips of bacon, cut into strips
1 tablespoon butter
1 large onion, chopped
1 garlic clove, finely chopped
2 tablespoons chopped fresh parsley
1 teaspoon fresh thyme leaves or
    ½ teaspoon dried thyme
1 pound tomatoes, skinned, seeded
    and chopped
⅔ cup dry vermouth or white wine
10 ounces potatoes, diced
1½–2 pounds skinless white fish fillets, cut
    into large chunks
salt and freshly ground black pepper
fresh flat leaf parsley sprig, to garnish

For the stock

8 ounces white fish trimmings, including
    heads and bones
2 tablespoons butter
1 shallot, finely chopped
1 leek, white part only, finely chopped
1 cup mushrooms, finely chopped
¼ cup dry white wine
2½ cups water
bouquet garni, consisting of 1 thyme
    sprig, 2 parsley sprigs and 1 bay leaf
small strip of dried orange peel

1 First make the stock. Put the fish trimmings in a large bowl, cover with cold water and set aside for 1–2 hours, then drain and chop into small pieces.

2 Melt the butter in a heavy saucepan, add the finely chopped shallot, leek and mushrooms and fry gently over low heat for 2–3 minutes, or until softened but not browned. Stir in the fish trimmings.

3 Add the wine and bring to a boil over high heat. Boil until reduced by half, then add the water and bring back to a boil. Skim the surface, add the bouquet garni and orange peel, lower the heat and simmer for 25 minutes. Strain the stock and set aside. Discard the vegetables, bouquet garni and orange peel.

4 Fry the bacon in a large saucepan over medium heat until lightly browned but not crisp, then remove the bacon and drain on paper towels.

5 Add the butter to the pan and gently fry the onion, stirring occasionally, for 3–5 minutes or until soft. Add the garlic, parsley and thyme and cook for 1 more minute, stirring constantly. Add the tomatoes, vermouth or white wine and the strained fish stock and bring to a boil.

6 Reduce the heat, cover and simmer the stew for about 15 minutes. Add the potatoes, cover again and simmer for another 10–12 minutes or until they are almost tender.

7 Add the chunks of fish and the bacon. Simmer gently, uncovered, for 5 minutes or until the fish is just cooked and the potatoes are tender. Adjust the seasoning, garnish with the flat leaf parsley and serve.

COOK'S TIP

It is worth taking the trouble to make fish stock.
Fish trimmings are usually very cheap and sometimes even free, but do make sure that they are fresh. It is best to avoid oily fish, such as mackerel or sardines, but virtually all types of white fish are suitable. Remove any roe and gills before cooking, as these will make the stock bitter. Fish heads, in particular, yield the greatest flavor and nutritional content, and bones are also useful.
Do not overlook the value of shrimp shells and heads, which, used on their own, make an aromatic and flavorful stock for poaching shellfish. They add a surprising amount of strength to a basic white fish stock, too.
Try experimenting with different types of fish; there is surprising variation in the flavor and body produced. The preparation and cooking take little time, and it is worth bearing in mind that fish stock does not benefit from prolonged cooking, which will result in a bitter taste.

Seafood Stew

"Soups"—really stews—of mixed fish and shellfish are specialties of all Mediterranean countries.

INGREDIENTS

Serves 6–8

3 tablespoons olive oil

1 medium onion, sliced

1 carrot, sliced

½ stalk celery, sliced

2 garlic cloves, chopped

1 can (14 ounces) plum tomatoes, chopped, with their juice

4 cups water

8 ounces raw shrimp, shelled and deveined (reserve the shells)

1 pound white fish bones and heads, gills removed

1 bay leaf

1 sprig fresh thyme, or ¼ teaspoon dried thyme leaves

4 black peppercorns

1½ pounds fresh mussels, in their shells, scrubbed and rinsed

1 pound fresh small clams, in their shells, scrubbed and rinsed

1 cup white wine

2¼ pounds mixed fish fillets, such as cod, monkfish, red mullet or hake, cut into chunks

3 tablespoons finely chopped fresh parsley

salt and freshly ground black pepper

rounds of French bread, toasted, to serve

1 Heat the oil in a medium-size saucepan. Add the onion and cook slowly until soft but not colored. Stir in the carrot and celery and cook for another 5 minutes. Add the garlic, the tomatoes and their juice and 1 cup water. Cook over medium heat for about 15 minutes, until the vegetables are soft. Purée in a food processor or pass through a food mill. Set aside.

2 Place the shrimp shells in a large saucepan with the fish bones and heads. Add the herbs, peppercorns and remaining water. Bring to a boil, reduce the heat, and simmer for 25 minutes, skimming off any scum that rises to the surface. Strain and pour into a pan with the tomato sauce. Season to taste.

3 Place the mussels and clams in a saucepan with the wine. Cover and steam until all the shells have opened. Discard any that do not open.

4 Lift the mussels and clams out and set aside. Filter the cooking liquid through a layer of paper towels and add it to the stock and tomato sauce mixture. Check the seasoning.

5 Bring the sauce to a boil. Add the fish and boil for 5 minutes. Stir in the mussels and clams and cook for another 2–3 minutes. Transfer the stew to a warmed casserole. Sprinkle with parsley, and serve with the toasted rounds of French bread.

Italian Fish Stew

Italians are renowned for enjoying good food, especially if it is shared with all the members of an extended family. This stew is a veritable feast of fish and seafood in a delicious tomato broth, suitable for a more modest family lunch.

INGREDIENTS

Serves 4

2 tablespoons olive oil

1 onion, thinly sliced

a few saffron threads

1 teaspoon dried thyme

large pinch of cayenne pepper

2 garlic cloves, finely chopped

2 cans (14 ounces each) peeled tomatoes, drained and chopped

¾ cup dry white wine

8 cups hot fish stock

12 ounces skinless white fish fillets, cut into pieces

1 pound monkfish, membrane removed, cut into pieces

1 pound mussels in the shell, scrubbed and "beards" removed

8 ounces small squid, cleaned and cut into rings

2 tablespoons chopped fresh basil or parsley

salt and freshly ground black pepper

thickly sliced bread, to serve

1 Heat the oil in a large heavy saucepan. Add the onion, saffron, thyme, cayenne pepper and salt, to taste. Stir well and cook over low heat for 8–10 minutes, until the onion is soft. Add the garlic and cook for another minute.

2 Stir in the tomatoes, wine and fish stock. Bring to a boil and boil for 1 minute, then reduce the heat and simmer gently for 15 minutes.

3 Add the white fish fillet and monkfish pieces to the pan and simmer gently over low heat for another 3 minutes.

4 Add the mussels and squid rings and simmer for about 2 minutes, until the mussels open. Discard any that remain closed. Stir in the basil or parsley and season to taste. Ladle into warmed soup bowls and serve with bread.

Ragoût of Shellfish with Sweet Scented Basil

Green curry paste is an integral part of Thai cooking and can be used to accompany other dishes made with fish or chicken. Curry pastes will keep for up to 3 weeks stored in an airtight container in the refrigerator.

INGREDIENTS

Serves 4–6

1 pound fresh mussels in their shells, scrubbed and with "beards" removed

¼ cup water

8 ounces medium squid

1⅔ cups canned coconut milk

1¼ cups chicken or vegetable stock

12 ounces monkfish, hoki or red snapper, skinned

5 ounces raw or cooked shrimp, peeled and deveined

4 scallops, sliced (optional)

4 ounces green beans, trimmed and cooked

¼ cup canned bamboo shoots, drained

1 ripe tomato, skinned, seeded, and roughly chopped

4 sprigs large-leaf basil, torn, and strips of fresh red chili, to garnish

rice, to serve (optional)

For the green curry paste

2 teaspoons coriander seeds

½ teaspoon caraway or cumin seeds

3–4 fresh green chilies, finely chopped

4 teaspoons superfine sugar

3-inch piece lemon grass

¾-in piece ginger, finely chopped

3 garlic cloves, crushed

4 shallots or 1 medium onion, finely chopped

¾-inch-square piece shrimp paste

1 cup cilantro leaves, finely chopped

3 tablespoons fresh mint or basil, finely chopped

½ teaspoon ground nutmeg

2 tablespoons vegetable oil

salt

1 Place the mussels in a large saucepan, add the water, cover and cook for 6–8 minutes, until the shells open. Take three-quarters of the mussels out of their shells and set aside. (Discard any that have not opened.) Strain the cooking liquid and set aside.

2 To prepare the squid, trim off the tentacles beneath the eye. Rinse under cold running water, discarding the gut. Remove the "quill" from inside the body and rub off the paper-thin skin. Cut the body open and score with a sharp knife. Cut into strips and set aside.

3 To make the green curry paste, dry-fry the coriander and caraway seeds in a wok to release their flavor. Grind the chilies with the sugar and 2 teaspoons salt in a mortar with a pestle or in a food processor to make a smooth paste. Combine the seeds from the wok with the chilies, add the lemon grass, ginger, garlic and shallots, then grind or process until smooth.

4 Add the shrimp paste, cilantro, mint or basil, nutmeg and vegetable oil to the food processor or mortar. Combine well.

5 Pour the coconut milk into a strainer. Pour the thin part of the milk, together with the chicken stock and the reserved mussel cooking liquid, into a wok. Reserve the coconut milk solids. Add 4–5 tablespoons of the green curry paste, according to taste. You can add more paste later, if you need to. Boil rapidly until the liquid has reduced completely.

6 Add the coconut milk solids, then add the squid and monkfish. Simmer for 15–20 minutes. Then add the shrimp, scallops and cooked mussels with the beans, bamboo shoots and tomato. Simmer for 2–3 minutes, transfer to a bowl and decorate with the basil and chilies. Serve with rice, if desired.

Haddock and Broccoli Stew

This is an easy, one-pot meal full of color and texture.

INGREDIENTS

Serves 4

4 scallions, sliced

1 pound new potatoes, diced

1¼ cups fish stock or water

1¼ cups milk

1 bay leaf

½ bunch broccoli florets, sliced

1 pound smoked haddock fillets, skinned

1 can (7 ounces) corn, drained

freshly ground black pepper

chopped scallions, to garnish

crusty bread, to serve

1 Place the scallions and potatoes in a large saucepan and add the stock or water, milk and bay leaf. Bring the mixture to a boil, then cover the pan and simmer for 10 minutes.

2 Add the broccoli to the pan. Cut the fish into bite-size chunks and add to the pan with the corn.

3 Season the stew well with freshly ground black pepper, then cover the pan and simmer for another 5 minutes or until the fish is cooked through. Remove the bay leaf and transfer to a serving dish. Scatter on the scallions and serve hot with crusty bread.

COOK'S TIP

When new potatoes are not available, old ones can be used, but choose a waxy variety that will not disintegrate.

Hoki Balls in Tomato Sauce

This quick meal is a good choice for young children, as you can guarantee no bones. Its low fat content also makes it an ideal dish for anyone on a low-fat or low-cholesterol diet. If desired, add a dash of chili sauce.

INGREDIENTS

Serves 4

1 pound hoki or other white fish
   fillets, skinned

¼ cup fresh whole wheat bread crumbs

2 tablespoons snipped chives or scallions

1 can (14 ounces) chopped tomatoes

2 ounces button mushrooms, sliced

salt and freshly ground black pepper

fresh chives, to garnish

1 Cut the fish fillets into large chunks and place in a food processor. Add the whole wheat bread crumbs and the chives or scallions. Season to taste with salt and pepper and process until the fish is finely chopped, but still has some texture left.

COOK'S TIP

Hoki is a good choice for this dish, but if it is not available, use cod, haddock or whiting instead.

2 Divide the fish mixture into about 16 even-size pieces, then mold them into balls with your hands.

3 Place the tomatoes and mushrooms in a large saucepan and cook over medium heat until boiling. Carefully add the fish balls, cover and simmer for about 10 minutes, until cooked. Serve hot, garnished with chives.